Virgo
24 August – 23 September

DID YOU PURCHASE THIS BOOK WITHOUT A COVER?
If you did, you should be aware it is **stolen property** as it was reported *unsold and destroyed* by a retailer. Neither the author nor the publisher has received any payment for this book.

All Rights Reserved including the right of reproduction in whole or in part in any form. This edition is published by arrangement with Harlequin Enterprises II B.V./S.à.r.l. The text of this publication or any part thereof may not be reproduced or transmitted in any form or by any means, electronic or mechanical, including photocopying, recording, storage in an information retrieval system, or otherwise, without the written permission of the publisher.

This book is sold subject to the condition that it shall not, by way of trade or otherwise, be lent, resold, hired out or otherwise circulated without the prior consent of the publisher in any form of binding or cover other than that in which it is published, and without a similar condition including this condition being imposed on the subsequent purchaser.

® and ™ are trademarks owned and used by the trademark owner and/or its licensee. Trademarks marked with ® are registered with the United Kingdom Patent Office and/or the Office for Harmonisation in the Internal Market and in other countries.

*First published in Great Britain 2008
by Harlequin Mills & Boon Limited,
Eton House, 18-24 Paradise Road, Richmond, Surrey TW9 1SR*

Copyright © Dadhichi Toth 2007, 2008 & 2009

ISBN: 978 0 263 86909 5

Typeset at Midland Typesetters Australia

Harlequin Mills & Boon policy is to use papers that are natural, renewable and recyclable products and made from wood grown in sustainable forests. The logging and manufacturing processes conform to the legal environmental regulations of the country of origin.

*Printed and bound in Spain
by Litografia Rosés S.A., Barcelona*

About
Dadhichi

Dadhichi is one of Australia's foremost astrologers, and is frequently seen on TV and in the media. He has the unique ability to draw from complex astrological theory to provide clear, easily understandable advice and insights for people who want to know what their future may hold.

In the 25 years that Dadhichi has been practising astrology, and conducting face and other esoteric readings, he has provided over 9,000 consultations. His clients include celebrities, political and diplomatic figures and media and corporate identities from all over the world.

Dadhichi's unique blend of astrology and face reading helps people fulfil their true potential. His extensive experience practising western astrology is complemented by his research into the theory and practice of eastern forms of astrology.

Dadhichi has been a guest on many Australian television shows and several of his political and worldwide forecasts have proved uncannily accurate. He has appeared on many of Australia's leading television networks and is a regular columnist for several Australian magazines.

His websites www.astrology.com.au, www.facereader.com and soulmate.com.au which attract hundreds of thousands of visitors each month, offer a wide variety of features, helpful information and services.

Dedicated to The Light of Intuition
Sri V. Krishnaswamy — mentor and friend

With thanks to Julie, Joram, Isaac and Janelle

Welcome from
Dadhichi

Dear Friend,

It's a pleasure knowing you're reading this, your astrological forecast for 2009. There's nothing more exciting than looking forward to a bright new year and considering what the stars have in store and how you might make the most of what's on offer in your life.

Apart from the anticipation of what I might predict will happen to you, of what I say about your upcoming luck and good fortune, remember that astrology is first and foremost a tool of personal growth, self-awareness and inner transformation. What 'happens to us' is truly a reflection of what we're giving out; the signals we are transmitting to our world, our universe.

The astrological adage of 'As above, so below' can also be interpreted in a slightly different way when I say 'As within, so without'! In other words, as hard as it is to believe, the world and our experiences of it, or our relationships and circumstances, good or bad, do tend to mirror our own belief systems and mental patterns.

It is for this reason that I thought I'd write a brief introductory note to remind you that the stars are pointers to your wonderful destiny and that you must work with them to realise your highest and most noble goals. The greatest marvel and secret is your own inner self! Astrology reveals these inner secrets of your character, which are the foundation of your life's true purpose.

What is about to happen to you this year is exciting, but what you *do* with this special power of knowledge, how you share your talents with others, and the way you truly enjoy each moment of your life is far more important than knowing *what* will happen. This is the key to a 'superior' kind of happiness. It will start to open up to you when you live in harmony with your true nature as shown by astrology.

I really hope you enjoy your coming twelve months, and gain new insights and fresh perspectives on your life through studying your 2009 horoscope. Here's hoping great success will be yours and health, love and happiness will follow wherever you go.

I leave you now with the words of a wise man, who once said:

> Sow a thought, and you reap an act;
> Sow an act, and you reap a habit;
> Sow a habit, and you reap a character;
> Sow a character, and you reap a destiny.
> Your thoughts are the architects of your destiny.

Warm regards, and may the stars shine brightly for you in 2009!

Your Astrologer,

Dadhichi Toth

Contents

The Virgo Identity 9

   Virgo: A Snapshot 10

Star Sign Compatibility 25

2009: The Year Ahead 49

2009: Month By Month Predictions 59

   January 60

   February 64

   March 68

   April 72

   May 76

   June 80

July	84
August	88
September	92
October	96
November	100
December	104

2009: Astronumerology 109

2009: Your Daily Planner 131

The Virgo Identity

VIRGO

True hope dwells on the possible, even when life seems to be a plot written by someone who wants to see how much adversity we can overcome. True hope responds to the real world, to real life; it is an active effort.

—Walter Anderson

Virgo: A Snapshot

Key Characteristics

Analytical, reserved, selfless, introverted, exacting, perfectionist, critical

Compatible Star Signs

Taurus, Capricorn, Cancer, Scorpio

Key Life Phrase

I serve

Life Goals

To create works of excellence that also inspire others

Platinum Assets

Selfless service, intuitive mind and tireless work ethic

Zodiac Totem

The Virgin

Zodiac Symbol

♍

Zodiac Facts

Sixth sign of the zodiac; mutable, barren, feminine, dry

THE VIRGO IDENTITY

Element

Earth

Famous Virgos

Richard Attenborough, Mother Teresa, Richard Gere, Shania Twain, Andy Roddick, Adam Sandler, Agatha Christie, Cameron Diaz, Bruce Springsteen, Bill Murray, Beyoncé, Goran Ivanisevic, H.G. Wells, Greta Garbo, Harry Connick Jr, Hugh Grant, Keanu Reeves, Queen Elizabeth I, Salma Hayek

Key to karma, spirituality and emotional balance

Your key words are 'I serve' and the challenge for you, Virgo, is to balance your desire to serve and your emotional needs. You must serve but remember that your view of what's best for someone else may not necessarily be the whole truth.

Your other key life phrase is 'I analyse'. Try to develop your intuitive, feeling nature as you are just as much an emotional being as you are an intellectual one.

Virgo: Your profile

Virgo, yours is the star sign of true perfectionism, diligence and first-class service. You are extremely conscious of how well everything should be done. But you're also critical about most things, especially your own character and this is what people sometimes misunderstand about you and think that you're impossible to please. This is just the way you are wired and your attention to detail and aspiration to excellence carries over into every aspect of your life, including the way you see yourself.

Everything has to be just right with you, Virgo, so you do have this unusual tendency to be particularly fastidious about your environment and the way you look. You have very high

VIRGO

standards and, unless others are able to meet these requirements of yours, they may find it extremely hard getting into your good books.

Cleanliness and hygiene are also some of your bugbears. There's nothing wrong with keeping clean and making sure your health is up to scratch, but for some Virgos, this can become an obsessive pastime and does seem rather odd to those who aren't quite as meticulous as you are.

You're an excellent critic and observer of human nature and the world around you. Your analysis of life and what goes on in it is usually quite correct, but try to curb your habit of finding fault with every little thing. This will be very annoying to your loved ones, who will find it hard meeting your expectations. Again, this tendency will be turned on yourself with the result that you may never be quite satisfied with your own work or who you are as a person. There's nothing wrong with you, Virgo: you're one of the good guys, remember that.

You have a wonderful broad base of knowledge, which means you're generally quite interesting to be with and you converse with anyone you happen to meet. You're always able to come up with impromptu solutions to the problems of others and this is another rather fascinating aspect of your personality.

Because you admire good service, you will also endeavour your best to provide first-class assistance to others. This is your primary motivation in life, which is why I say your keywords are 'I serve'. If someone asks you to do something, you like to do it properly without cutting corners and rushing the job. Making sure that every detail is attended to, you're impressive even in the most mundane tasks.

Disorganisation is abhorrent to you, which is why you are neat and tidy and will always have a diary with you. Are you one of those Virgos who is always making lists to make sure that you don't leave something out? I hope you're not a person who has a briefcase or handbag full of lists and never quite

THE VIRGO IDENTITY

finishes what's on that list! Organise your time a little better so that you don't run yourself ragged.

Virgos are cautious characters and don't like to rush things. You are also shy and unassuming, but this is only because you like to analyse something or someone before committing yourself to an opinion. Virgos aren't the sort of people who jump to conclusions, so your judgements are usually correct and the outcome satisfactory. You may take longer than most to achieve your goals, but you prefer to finish the race a little more slowly than to make an error.

Loyalty and honour are particularly important to you in any type of relationship and others will soon realise this as they get to know you. You give of yourself 100 per cent and expect the same level of integrity from those around you. This could also become something that dominates your relationships and you must be careful not to become habituated to testing your friends to see whether they are genuine. This will make them feel as if they're under the magnifying glass for every little thing and it will alienate them. Try to trust people more, which will help you unwind and enjoy life.

Three classes of Virgo

Virgos generally prefer to remain in the background rather than having the spotlight turned on them, but this applies particularly if you were born between the 24th of August and the 3rd of September. You hate to be the centre of attention. If someone points the finger at you and you're singled out in a crowd, you'll turn a bright shade of red. You're quite happy to remain anonymous, be one of the quiet achievers in life, and prefer to concentrate on the details without too much fanfare.

Those of you born between the 4th and 14th of September have an incredible amount of mental clarity and can really understand things that most others overlook. Yes, you are a rational individual, but your thinking is as quick as lightning and you should have no problem using this to gain success in life. Try to keep a sense of humour about you, though.

You have a useful and innocent quality about you if you're born between the 15th and the 23rd of September. Your co-ruler is Venus and it infuses you with a sensual energy. If you are born during these dates you'll remain young at heart and like to live your life to the fullest. You're a fun Virgo to be around.

Virgo role model: Richard Attenborough

Richard epitomises Virgo through his selfless efforts to raise the world's awareness of nature, animals and their connections to it. In his filmmaking you can see his attention to detail, which is the hallmark of almost all Virgo personalities. You too exhibit many of these same traits as Richard.

Virgo: The light side

Few people are as loyal in friendship as you. This is one of your most admirable traits. When people first meet you, you are aloof and cool, but this is because Virgos are inherently shy. They could even go so far as to think you're looking down your nose at them. But when they get to know you, you endear yourself to them and share the deeper side of your character.

Service is one of your most shining qualities, and whether the job is large or small, you see it as an opportunity to create perfection and help others achieve their goals, too. You selflessly give of yourself to help others reach their goals as you gain a quiet, secret pleasure through this.

You have wonderful ideas and also have a knack of conveying facts and figures to others who are not as adept at grasping concepts. This makes you an excellent teacher or trainer.

You are capable of seeing diverse views in an argument. This makes you impartial and a good judge or mediator when

THE VIRGO IDENTITY

it comes to solving problems. You are seen as a fair individual and your ruling is respected.

Virgo: The shadow side

Your brilliant mind sometimes gets itself into trouble because of your tendency to be overly critical of both others and yourself. This must be your biggest challenge in life—knowing how to balance faultfinding with constructive criticism.

Your achievements are never quite satisfactory to you because you always feel as if you could have done better. Even if others praise you and genuinely believe you're doing a good job, you never accept this, do you? Give yourself some credit! Be a little more gentle on yourself.

Virgo is clean and fastidious. Some are even obsessively compulsive. You may not go to this extreme in your hygiene, but the tidiness you impose on others can sometimes alienate you from them. You need to learn the art of relaxation and not worry about things not being in their place.

This outer attention to detail, criticism and hygiene is masking some subtle insecurities in your nature, which need to be addressed in due course. If not, this attitude will no doubt act as an obstacle to happy and fulfilling relationships.

By overcoming your tense and highly critical approach you'll find your life so much more satisfying.

Virgo woman

Virgo is a feminine sign and therefore women born under the rulership of this zodiac star reflect many of the traditional values associated with the fairer sex. You are committed to serving, have a love of family, and your selflessness is obvious to most who know you. But this doesn't for a minute mean that you will be a doormat for anyone who wants to take advantage of you, that's for sure.

VIRGO

As a modern-day woman you are progressive and committed to doing your duty as best you can. You are clean, efficient and hard-working, and don't expect to be treated any differently from anyone else. Your impartial attitude in the world is a welcome change from the façades that people put up in everyday relationships. You are transparent, honest and straightforward in your dealings and, even if you are complex by nature, you try not to let this interfere with your practical affairs.

At first glance others are likely to misinterpret what they see when they meet you. You're quiet and unassuming in style but your insights and careful observation of others will soon give them a rude shock when you reveal your true opinions about them. As soon as you feel comfortable and more relaxed in their company, your very strong-willed and opinionated nature will come to the forefront with full force.

You have an incredibly deductive mind and love to communicate your ideas. This is one of the great strengths of Virgo. You have factual knowledge but also the natural intuition that goes with the feminine signs of the zodiac. Research and making sure you understand your chosen topic is what makes you such a wealth of knowledge both in your work and socially. When you take up a subject you do so with much intensity and the desire to understand the topic completely in an expert manner.

The feminine grace that you bring to any relationship or friendship makes you attractive and desirable. Your beauty is sometimes intangible but nevertheless palpable and undeniable. Because you have a genuine desire to help others and to be a true friend, you are sometimes viewed with suspicion by others who can't seem to understand what your motive is. Unbeknown to them, you are just one of the good guys simply trying to lead a good life and give back something to others.

You're always there to help a friend and the best adviser when the going gets tough for them. Because your ruler, Mercury,

THE VIRGO IDENTITY

has the ability to communicate and solve intellectual problems, your psychic flashes and innate wisdom come up with the solution to many problems. This makes you greatly appreciated wherever you go.

The female Virgo is a nervous, highly strung type of person but, strangely, you will gain strength in times of great challenge. It is usually only the smaller details of life that ruffle your feathers. You need to take things more slowly and not get too uptight about the inconsequential aspects of day-to-day living. By speaking about how you feel and sharing your inner thoughts with a close friend, you'll feel much better and able to bring out the best side of your character.

Family life and nurturing children comes easy to you due to the fact that service is your second name. Looking after the needs of your partner, your children and other relatives or friends will allow you to express this natural tendency to love selflessly and unconditionally. You're a woman through and through.

Virgo man

Virgo men have a distinct advantage over others. You have one of the most penetrating minds with an equally keen eye for any sort of detail work. Your perception is sharp and you don't miss a trick. Analysis is such an ingrained part of your character that it probably annoys you when you want to turn off your brain but can't. Your curiosity is the primary force behind your desire to understand anything and everything.

You shine the torchlight of inquisitiveness onto your relationships, too. You have an extraordinary insight into human nature and love to study people. It's a hobby, actually. Your clever observations lead you to understand people easily and this is something you didn't learn from books or teachers; rather, you've had this ability since you can remember. You live most of your life in the intellectual

VIRGO

realm, analysing, scrutinising and deducting so many things. Try letting go and relaxing for this will give you the well deserved rest you need.

You have a dual nature and turn the different shades of your character on and off when it suits you. This can make it rather hard for people to understand you. You are a chameleon and confuse others with your changeable moods. Virgo, like Gemini, is ruled by Mercury, the dual-natured planet. You are as much a twin as Gemini but not quite so obviously. There is a hidden side to your temperament. You will show this side of your personality only to those whom you consider worthy.

In your romantic life, you are cool in the way you express your feelings. If your partner demands more passion from you it may be difficult for them to understand your ways. You express your love through service, providing security and sharing your time and energy rather than making outward demonstrative shows of affection. You are really quite an affectionate person but need to feel that the circumstances are just right for sharing your love and sex.

Virgo child

Children of Virgo tend to worry a lot, which is why you'll need to be extra loving to them. Highly strung and nervous by nature they are however peaceful and generally shy until they develop confidence, usually as they grow a little older.

They have brilliant little minds and are curious about everything in life. Because of their ruling planet, Mercury, they are quick to learn and also partial to good humour and jokes. You will do plenty of laughing with your Virgo child.

Young Virgo children mature quite early and you'll see this in the skills they exhibit, even in preschool. Take the time to help develop your child's mind and imagination as they are specially gifted with many talents—both practical and artistic.

THE VIRGO IDENTITY

Give them the time and space to nurture their interests because pushing them will only serve to make them even more volatile.

It's hard to turn off the young Virgo mind, but you must insist that they have a daily rest so that they can recharge their little intellectual batteries on a regular basis. They tend to have too many irons in the fire. This tendency to overwork can be a considerable strain on their nervous systems and so make sure you assist them in developing robust health.

Most Virgo children are delicate and fragile physically so pay strict attention to their diet, hygiene and other aspects of their health. They will let you know how they feel in any case as Virgo is the natural sign of health and these kids do tend to concern themselves with their health to the extreme. In fact, some of them become little hypochondriacs, worrying excessively about every little ache and pain. You will need to show your love by relieving them of their concerns and reassuring them that everything is quite all right.

Virgo children also take time to warm to the social groups at school. Don't push them too hard as they will come around in time and first need to feel totally comfortable with the many different characters they come in contact with. Social life is important to them and will give them the chance to show off their astounding abilities. When their friends discover that they are versatile personalities, however, they will become the centre of attention of their peer group and may even take the lead.

Romance, love and marriage

It must be rather embarrassing to have a virgin as your zodiac totem! One could think that because of this 'virginality' you might be cold, prudish and probably anything but romantic, warm-hearted and demonstrative in relationships. This is one of those age-old inaccuracies that has crept into astrological folklore and been presented to the world as gospel truth.

VIRGO

To enhance your romantic opportunities, you must first eliminate one small character trait that is probably holding you back: making too much of minor personality flaws in people who are likely to be prospective lovers or at least great friends over time. You tend to get bogged down with the details of people's characteristic weaknesses because of your very high standards. In some ways love is a subtle test of the other person's capabilities and ability to satisfy you. My main piece of advice is simply just to enjoy your relationships, have a good time, and just allow your friendships to mature naturally.

On the upside, you are a very straightforward person and your matter-of-fact attitude leaves no doubt in the minds of your perspective partners as to how honest you are. You always call a spade a spade and your genuineness is one of your most endearing qualities.

When someone becomes involved with you they must understand that the practical affairs of your life are as important to you as caring for your emotional needs. You reciprocate in exactly the same way you receive and, although not passionate in the usual sense, you will slowly warm to someone who can prove their worth on these initial matters.

One of the other reasons you may find it hard to get your romance off the ground is that you are generally a shy type of person and are not quick in coming forward to showcase your talents. You prefer to watch and wait and play the analytical game rather than competitively going after what you perceive to be a 'good catch'. Until you develop a reasonable level of comfort with someone, you are also likely to remain somewhat cool and aloof. Once that level of trust has been gained you openly display your warmth and affection.

Due to the rulership of your star sign by Mercury, humour and role-playing will play an important part in your love life. That person who happens to be the lucky recipient of your love

THE VIRGO IDENTITY

should get ready to have plenty of comical episodes as part of a life of love with you. If you find the right individual who has an intellectual appreciation for you as well as a good sense of humour, you will be extremely fulfilled emotionally.

Mercury is a youthful planet, which shows that people born under your star sign rarely subscribe to the view that one should grow old gracefully. You're able to keep your relationships alive with a playful and adventurous attitude. Your partner will definitely appreciate this aspect of your character. Many who happen to be born under Virgo appear to be a lot younger than their age. In fact, I have noted several of my clients finally marrying men who are younger than themselves because of their young and great-looking appearance.

Communication will be high on the agenda of your love life and you need a lover who has brains as well as an attractive body. Intelligence, wit and an all-round general knowledge are just some of the qualities you look for in a partner whom you consider a worthwhile soulmate. If a lover turns on your mind, they will have a much better chance of turning you on physically, too. You respect people who work hard and develop their skills and wisdom on a practical level. You would like to think that this feeling would be mutual. Your relationships will be based primarily on this one point.

Sexuality is never a frivolous matter to Virgo and you usually reserve this for someone you truly love. Once you decide that you want an intimate relationship, you'll give 100 per cent of yourself to them. Strangely, hygiene, purity and appropriate timing are an essential part of your views on love and sex and are part of your high standard in relationships. Just don't allow them to become obsessive traits.

When you marry you will provide emotional and sexual satisfaction to your partner, and usually marry with a view to long-term commitment. Because service is your middle name, your lucky partner will realise just how blessed they are to have

VIRGO

someone like you in their life tending to their each and every need. You understand that this is what makes true love a reality and bond that is not temporary but will last eternally.

Health, wellbeing and diet

Virgo is naturally linked to health in astrology and consequently, many Virgos take an interest in wellbeing and related topics. You can integrate health into your schedule quite easily. By doing so you can overcome sensitivities and allergic reactions to food and other environmental factors to which you are predisposed.

You're prone to nervous disorders due to your ruler, Mercury, governing this part of the body. Your emotional and mental reactions to the people you live and work with will have a marked impact upon your physical vitality and health. It is therefore particularly important for you to maintain a peaceful attitude and don't do anything that puts you into stressful situations that can otherwise be avoided. Work in particular is one area where many Virgos overdo it and this is a case in point. Work moderately and always only at something you love doing. This too will ensure you enjoy continuing health.

Your skin, lower intestines, nervous system and waist area are also governed by your sign of Virgo. Diet and exercise are the important determinants as to how well these parts of your body will function. To a large extent the food you eat will generally determine how healthy you are.

Dietary issues have a marked influence on how well you feel and in the long run how you might avoid physical discomfort and disease. Because Virgo comes under the category of earth astrologically, anything grown in the earth will augment your health. Vegetables, salads and any leafy green vegetables are great for you and will help strengthen you against allergies. Please note that it's best not to overcook your vegetables and where possible try to eat them raw.

THE VIRGO IDENTITY

Because your digestive system is a little more sensitive than most, eat small meals and chew your food well. Always dine in a relaxed atmosphere with people whose company you enjoy. This will help you on your path to physical well-being.

There is the tendency in you to be worried about your health, even when there's nothing particularly wrong with you. Don't be too preoccupied with yourself and, if you do tend to be a little anxious, calming herbs such as skullcap, camomile, vervain and valerian root are ideally suited to the Virgo temperament and will help nourish your body as well. Always remember to include supplements such as vitamins B, C and E along with whole grains such as rye, wheat and barley in your diet.

Work

Virgo has a first-rate mind and has no trouble finding employment in any chosen line of work. However, because different star signs do possess strengths in different areas, it's worth mentioning your brilliant and deductive mind, which offers you ample opportunities in intellectual fields.

Being a born organiser you're able to apply many of your abilities to your chosen profession and your detail-oriented methods will win favour with your co-workers and employers because you like to do the job properly, down to the most exacting standards.

Some of the best jobs for Virgo are those which involve number crunching such as accounting, mathematics or the banking and investment fields. Your finicky mind likes to know that one plus one does indeed equal two. As mentioned earlier, the medical profession and any health or hygiene-related fields work well for you because this star sign is so naturally linked to the issues of health, vitality and also disease.

VIRGO

Being appreciated for a job well done is more important to you than the money earned from work. Because service is your number one priority, this will be your focus and will result in you becoming an expert in any field you choose. Customer service will therefore also be an area you might consider.

A significant requirement of your work is that those you work with must be orderly and tidy, otherwise this will worry you and detract from your work satisfaction. However, you mustn't impose your perfectionism on others as this will backfire and cause you no end of problems. At some point you have to learn that others have their own way of doing things and it's simply best to put your head down and get on with your own job.

Your lucky days

Your luckiest days are Wednesdays, Fridays and Saturdays.

Your lucky numbers

Remember that the forecasts given later in the book will help you optimise your chances of winning. Your lucky numbers are:

5, 14, 23, 32, 41, 50

6, 15, 24, 33, 42, 51

8, 17, 26, 35, 44, 53

Your destiny years

Your most important years are 5, 14, 23, 32, 41, 50, 68, 77 and 86.

VIRGO

Star Sign Compatibility

VIRGO

Nine-tenths of wisdom is appreciation. Go find somebody's hand while there's time.

—Dale Dauten

Romantic compatibility

How compatible are you with your current partner, lover or friend? Did you know that astrology can reveal a whole new level of understanding between people simply by looking at their star sign and that of their partner? In this chapter I'd like to share some special insights that will help you better appreciate your strengths and challenges using Sun sign compatibility.

The Sun reflects your drive, willpower and personality. The essential qualities of two star signs blend like two pure colours producing an entirely new colour. Relationships, similarly, produce their own emotional colours when two people interact. The following is a general guide to your romantic prospects with others and how, by knowing the astrological 'colour' of each other, the art of love can help you create a masterpiece.

When reading the following I ask you to remember that no two star signs are ever *totally* incompatible. With effort and compromise, even the most 'difficult' astrological matches can work. Don't close your mind to the full range of life's possibilities! Learning about each other and ourselves is the most important facet of astrology.

Each star sign combination is followed by the elements of those star signs and the result of their combining. For instance, Aries is a fire sign and Aquarius is an air sign, and this combination produces a lot of 'hot air'. Air feeds fire, and fire warms air. In fact, fire requires air. However, not all air and fire combinations work. I have included information about the different birth periods within each star sign and this will throw even more light on your prospects for a fulfilling love life with any star sign you choose.

Good luck in your search for love, and may the stars shine upon you in 2009!

Compatibility quick reference guide

Each of the twelve star signs has a greater or lesser affinity with one another. The quick reference guide on page 28 will show you who's hot and who's not so hot as far as your relationships are concerned.

VIRGO + ARIES
Earth + Fire = Lava

How will the prudent Virgo handle the hot and sizzling Aries, which seems to be so vastly different in temperament? With great difficulty, it appears. You see, Aries is at the other end of the spectrum in the way they express themselves compared to you. Aries with their hot and outgoing personality is always on the go, physically mobile and often challenging at the best of times. You, on the other hand are cooler, earthy and more practical in your ways.

The fast and furious nature of the Aries born irritates you in many ways because they often don't appear to be thinking through their actions. You like to take your time to think things through at a slower pace so that you don't make errors of judgement. Aries is by nature very impulsive. If you happen to be a dynamic and speculative Virgo, you might like to take a chance with Aries, however.

Because yours is the earth element, you like to have your feet planted firmly on the ground and like to know precisely where your money and security is. This is also the case with Aries but they are much more gung-ho in approach, causing you some insecurity, to say the least.

Quick reference guide: Horoscope compatibility between signs (percentage)

	Aries	Taurus	Gemini	Cancer	Leo	Virgo	Libra	Scorpio	Sagittarius	Capricorn	Aquarius	Pisces
Aries	60	65	65	65	90	45	70	80	90	50	55	65
Taurus	60	70	70	80	70	90	75	85	50	95	80	85
Gemini	70	70	75	60	80	75	90	60	75	50	90	50
Cancer	65	80	60	75	70	75	60	95	55	45	90	50
Leo	90	70	80	70	85	75	65	75	95	45	70	90
Virgo	45	90	75	70	75	70	80	85	70	95	70	75
Libra	70	75	90	60	65	80	80	90	80	85	50	70
Scorpio	80	85	60	95	75	85	85	85	80	85	95	50
Sagittarius	90	50	75	55	95	70	80	65	85	55	60	95
Capricorn	50	95	50	45	45	95	85	60	55	85	60	75
Aquarius	55	80	90	70	70	50	95	60	60	70	80	85
Pisces	65	85	50	90	75	70	50	95	75	85	55	80

STAR SIGN COMPATIBILITY

However, Aries is exciting and this might just be something that attracts you to them. You probably envy those people who are able to project themselves more spontaneously than you do and perhaps you see this as a perfect opportunity to learn the art of self-confidence. In fact, they will happily encourage you to express more of yourself. This can be fun if you're able to let go a little more.

Both of you are hard-working and industrious, even though the way you work is also strikingly in contrast to each other. Unless Aries exercises patience and lets you do things with greater diligence, this will be a problem as they like to get to the finishing line as quickly as possible. You have a more cautious attitude.

Virgo is passionate but not as overtly as Aries so this combination in the bedroom needs time for intimacy to develop. The primal and less-than-sensitive reactions of Aries will be a turn-off to you. Your lovemaking could become an educational experience. If Aries is an intelligent sort of person who enjoys communication, then the prognosis is much better.

You are well suited to those born between 11 and 20 April because they have a connection with Jupiter, which regulates that zone of your horoscope associated with marriage. You will be attracted to them physically and enjoy an intellectual rapport together. You'll find them quite intelligent.

Aries born between 31 March and 10 April are quite strong in their opinions and may not like your criticism of them, irrespective of how constructive it is. This is not a particularly good match.

A relationship with Aries born between 21 and 30 March is physical and sexual. They are strongly driven and this may be hard for you to adjust to. Business with them could, however, have some positive outcomes.

VIRGO + TAURUS

Earth + Earth = Solid ground

The chemistry between Virgo and Taurus is undeniable. This is one of those combinations that works and without too much effort on either part. The reason for this is that astrologically both signs fall under the earth element. Similar elements naturally get on well so that the compatibility between you will be quite good physically, emotionally and mentally. Similar elements have a far greater chance of surviving the rocky road of relationship than most other star signs.

Both of you have a leaning towards the practical affairs of life and you'll appreciate this fact within each other. Material security is high on your list of priorities so that both of you will generally be heading in the same direction. You feel very comfortable that your ideals are the same, particularly financial ones.

You will both make each other feel secure and therefore the future prospects for your relationship are good overall. Unlike most other relationships you may not even need to go through the initial trauma of pulling each other into line with your monetary philosophies. You'll both naturally feel as if there is a mutual understanding.

Taurus is hard-working like you and, although not quite as much a perfectionist as yourself, likes to do the job well. But they are a little slower than you so at times they may try your patience. You are also a little more nervous about the outcome of things whereas many born under Taurus are quite easy-going. This could work in your favour if you slip into the Taurean pace of things.

Your communication is lively and very much on the same wavelength. You also have similar interests such as art, fashion, music and finally, wining and dining. If there are differences in your personalities, there is ample common interest to overcome this.

STAR SIGN COMPATIBILITY

There's a strong link romantically between you so I can safely predict your pleasure ratio will be high. You sexually balance and stimulate each other and this is another area that should bring you great satisfaction as a couple. You may need to spend a little more time creatively stimulating Taurus, who can be a little slow off the mark when it comes to initiating intimate moments.

If your Taurus partner is born between 30 April and 10 May you have a common denominator, Mercury, which partially influences them. This means that your connection will be strong and vital and you'll see much of yourself in each other. You'll find it very easy to talk about almost anything with them and vice versa. I see a great deal of pleasure resulting from a relationship with them.

Get ready for some exciting times with natives of Taurus born between 21 and 29 April. Venus, the planet of love, hints of an amorous association, which offers you both a rewarding partnership for years to come.

Taurus born between 11 and 21 May might turn out to be a little lacklustre in your opinion. This is due to the influence of Saturn, which is very reserved by nature. This is not the best of matches if you're looking for someone who is going to stimulate you and demonstrate their affection. You need someone who can reciprocate in a mutual partnership.

VIRGO + GEMINI
Earth + Air = Dust

Mercury, the communicator, is at the heart of both your star signs, but in Gemini it is not driven to perfect and deepen their knowledge as much as Virgo is. Therefore, the mind of Gemini might appear a little too shallow or superficial to you. You mustn't pass judgement too early as many Geminis develop a taste for deeper discussion in due course.

VIRGO

Gemini is the master multi-tasker. They have 1001 irons in the fire at any given moment and could drive you to distraction because you prefer more focus with clear objectives defined before you become involved. You secretly admire their capacity to enjoy doing so much, even if they appear to be going around in circles at times.

There's a strong correlation between domestic and family activities for Virgo and Gemini. You can make their home life much rosier and therefore living together will bring you a certain amount of satisfaction, notwithstanding the ad hoc approach to their daily living and lifestyle. In this matter, however, there are also some significant adjustments that will have to be made for you to get the living arrangement right. Time and patience will give you both the right balance.

You can give Gemini a strong sense of stability by anchoring them to a more practical daily regime, which can help rein in their scattered personalities. By the same token, don't smother them or try to control them too much or you might just see their light-hearted and humorous personalities evaporate before your very eyes. Be gentle in your criticisms and keep your discussions light-hearted, at least in the first stages of the relationship. You don't want to scare them away with too much heavy duty intellectual stuff.

As far as your lovemaking is concerned, Gemini, which is ruled by playful Mercury, will excite and stimulate you to explore different avenues thereby bringing you closer together. It's probably not the most striking sexual combination but one that, with a little mutual affection, will grow with time.

You may have already chosen your Gemini partner and have high expectations of them being your romantic soulmate and, if they happen to be born between 22 May and 1 June, then you may have hit the jackpot. They are indeed quite well suited to you and are particularly stimulating socially, bringing to any gathering a wealth of conversation with ample humour as well.

Geminis born between 2 and 12 June are influenced by Venus and the sign of Taurus so you'll find your relationship with them is also quite inspiring as your conversations will reach new levels. They are also financially stimulating to you so there could be a business arrangement that prospers under your partnership.

When you choose a relationship with a Gemini born between 13 and 21 June you are opening up a Pandora's box because Aquarius and Uranus will bring you unexpected delights and surprises. This can also forecast some challenges that you must be prepared to deal with if you commit yourself to them.

VIRGO + CANCER
Earth + Water = Mud

Both of you are sensitive individuals, being female signs of the zodiac. The feminine aspects of sensitivity, intuition and nurturing come easily to you and a relationship with Cancer will result in a mutual sharing of these noble human traits. Love between you will flow naturally. This is one of those relationships that has a good prospect of success even if you have some minor differences in your personalities.

There's a great deal of imagination in the Virgo and Cancer combination. This is because Cancer is ruled by the Moon, which is both creative and loving. It's pretty hard to beat the caring qualities of a Cancer partner. They will tend to your each and every need with true, unconditional love. You really relate to this and will want to mirror their actions by doing the same for them.

The two of you can be great friends and find satisfaction in each other's company. You could meet through some social engagement or a mutual friend. Social life will be loads of fun for both of you, but on a personal note, Cancer, who is

VIRGO

extremely volatile emotionally, will cause you to feel drained if this becomes a habitual pattern. Brainpower may not be the solution in a relationship of this type and will even have you pulling your hair out occasionally.

You are a positive influence on each other and can be better people for having met. Your personalities are truly compatible so there's not much of a downside to this relationship. Remain positive and focus on each other's needs rather than your own. Cancer will offer you domestic stability and happiness.

Because Cancer is hypersensitive, your impromptu comments may be taken personally even when you don't intend them to cut. Try to remain alert to the body signals of your Cancer partner as this will give you an insight into how better to deal with them. You can also use this knowledge to develop your level of intimacy. Don't be so demanding in the bedroom and Cancer will provide you the satisfaction you desire.

You can be a great friend and lover with Cancers born between 22 June and 3 July. You feel great in each other's company and this warmth will spill over into your social arena; through additional friendships the bonds of your own love will strengthen greatly. You are a great support to each other and, even if times are hard or discouraging, you'll find your Cancer mate a rock-solid support.

A long-lasting relationship is also possible with any Cancer born between 14 and 23 July. There is great physical compatibility between you and they also provide you with a sense of emotional satisfaction. You'll want to spend more time with them as you get to know them.

Cancers born between 4 and 13 July are not the usual run-of-the-mill people. They are extremely sensitive and intuitive and need to be handled with extreme care due to their spiri-

VIRGO + LEO
Earth + Fire = Lava

You both bring very different and unique energies to a Virgo–Leo romance. Your strong and inquisitive personality, along with Leo's dramatic and showy style, makes for a strong statement socially. The Virgo element of earth and fiery solar Leo mix produces a compelling match.

You will have to contend with Leo, who likes to be out in front. Fortunately you have no problem standing in their shadow as long as you have the occasional chance to let your own brilliance shine forth. This is because sacrifice and service are second nature to you and you'll enjoy watching Leo revel in the adulation of friends. If, however, Leo takes this for granted and doesn't learn to play the game of give and take, the relationship will stall.

Leo is a dominating star sign whereas you have a tendency to nitpick and this could be a cause of contention. Give each other space to be who you are and things should work quite well. Leo will be happy to accept the odd Virgo swipe at their personality, but you must also understand that they are opinionated characters who don't like being proved wrong. If you know you are correct, sharpen your diplomatic skills when you choose to point out the error of their ways.

Leo is probably a little less concerned with counting the pennies, which will cause you some concerns if you are one of those security conscious Virgos. Some Leos are spendthrifts and this will unhinge you. Finding a balance between your needs and their desires will be a challenge.

VIRGO

You must also feel confident that Leo isn't taking you for granted or using your generous nature to further their own selfish ends. Compromise and more compromise—this will be one of the secrets of success in a Virgo–Leo relationship.

Between the sheets, Leo will warm the cockles of your heart. But fire signs are more spontaneous than earth signs. You need to go with the flow of the creative Leo and learn the art of abandonment, which is the secret of true sexual pleasure. Leo is one of the star signs that can fulfil you.

There's a strong attraction for Leos born between 24 July and 4 August. They can bring a shy Virgo out of their shell and show them how to live a life of joy and creative happiness. They also have the uncanny knack of being able to calm your spirit.

A long-lasting relationship is likely with those born between 5 and 14 August. This combination has the blessings of Jupiter and materially you will prosper together. These Leos will be quite attracted to you.

The same can't be said for a relationship with Leos born between 15 and 23 August because Mars, an inimical planet to you, has a strong influence over them. This can create many problems, arguments and tension.

VIRGO + VIRGO
Earth + Earth = Solid ground

So, it looks like you've met your star twin? It will be like looking in a mirror when you connect with another Virgo. Both of you have very exacting and at times demanding minds so you'll be very much challenged in this romantic combination.

Because you both aspire to perfection, you may soon learn what it's like when you demand and expect too much of others who are not able to meet these expectations. Your Virgo partner will give you a clear insight into how this feels. As long as you keep an air of humour about your criticisms of each other, the relationship has a good chance of working.

Without expecting too much from each other, you have a great opportunity to enjoy the journey of love with your Virgo partner. Be gently encouraging to each other through your wonderful way of communicating and this can be a fulfilling partnership.

You are both driven by exactly the same material and professional goals, so this can be a good working relationship, financially and practically. Your life philosophies also follow similar lines and you'll feel an empathy with each other because of this. Making sure that the job is done well and that your future security is not left to chance makes you feel comfortable with each other. There is a lot of mutual support in this love affair.

Your home life is equally important and you will both work towards creating a safe haven that is tidy, pleasing to the eye and comfortable as well as functional. This sounds like the perfect nest for a family, doesn't it? And, Virgos do take pride in their families by looking after each and every need of their partners and young ones as well.

In your moments of intimacy and lovemaking, you'll have a similar approach and respect each other's need for good taste and sensitivity. You are emotional but this is not immediately obvious. With another Virgo it will be easier for you to feel understood and you will therefore open your heart readily. This can be very stimulating sexually, believe it or not.

By far your best compatibility is with a Virgo who is born between 24 August and 2 September. They have a clearer insight into your motivation and you likewise understand what turns them on. You are very tuned in to each other.

A more serious relationship takes place if you enter into romance with Virgos born between 3 and 12 September. They have a strong craving for the finer things in life and their tastes are quite expensive. It depends on who the breadwinner is and, if that is you, you may be working long hours to fulfil their needs.

If you choose a love affair with those born between 13 and 23 September this is not a bad match, either. Destiny will bring you together and this relationship will also be stable due to the fact that Taurus and Venus have an influence on them.

VIRGO + LIBRA
Earth + Air = Dust

The Virgo with Libra combination is probably a mixed bag, astrologically speaking. On the one hand your ruling planets Mercury and Venus respectively happen to be bosom buddies in the zodiac, but there are still significant differences that need to be addressed if you want to have a long-term relationship

Your social attitudes are very different but can still work if you're able to be considerate enough of each other's personalities. Libra is an outgoing but often changeable character and you prefer someone who knows their own mind and isn't so indecisive on every single matter. But they can indeed seduce you due to their lovely social and fair-minded attitude.

Libra is not averse to hearing what you have to say about them, even if you're pointing out their faults. Because they are interested in justice and self-improvement, they will actually be 100 per cent attentive to your advice. But they too may have some of their own opinions about you, so be prepared to accept their gripes gracefully.

Libra likes to play the field and may not be quite as committed to a relationship with you. The more you try to play the game of mental gymnastics to justify why you may be the one for them, the more distant you may find them. Try to enjoy their company and make them laugh and you'll win their hearts. Expanding your social circle will also make them feel as if you're on the same page as them. They love an ever-increasing circle of friends.

Libra loves sexuality and the idea of love and romance. Give them plenty of that and you will possess them. Talking about how you feel in a relationship will also make them feel you are caring and worthy of their time and devotion. They are great communicators, like you.

There are some differences with Librans born between 14 and 23 October. Less than conservative in their ways, you may find that you need to make too many adjustments to be with them, which compromises your own standards.

There is a better opportunity for a long-lasting relationship with Librans born between 4 and 13 October because they have the added influence of Aquarius, making them sexually provocative. Being progressive and experimental in love is important to them, so I hope you're prepared to try something a little out of the ordinary if you choose a relationship with them. Virgo is always open to learning new things, so why not give it a go?

Librans born between 24 September and 3 October can love you in just the way you want to be loved. They have an additional dose of Venus energy, which makes them natural lovers who want to share their body and their minds with that special person. Perhaps that is you and, if it is, this relationship will flow smoothly, giving you both many happy times together.

VIRGO + SCORPIO
Earth + Water = Mud

Virgo and Scorpio are able to achieve a lot on a material level but only do so because they are capable of being great friends wanting to support each other mutually in the process.

VIRGO

Scorpio is intellectual and philosophical and this will fascinate you. Their magnetic appeal is hard to resist and there is something about you that also attracts them. There's no doubt a relationship between you and Scorpio gets the green light. I see mental compatibility for you and this is important because once the sexual excitement has waned, it's nice to know you will still have something else going for you.

On the topic of sex, Scorpio can be a little more demanding than you would care for. If you can get into the swing of their intense and passionate sexual habits your relationship with them has an even greater chance of survival. You must understand that they are the most sexual of the star signs and need nourishment on that level. It's a big ask, Virgo.

Scorpio is dominant, confrontational, sarcastic and critical. This is in contrast to the way you make your point, which is always more tactful. You'll wonder when Scorpio is going to take the hint and be a little more considerate when criticising you! At the end of the day, you must both accept each other, understanding that humans come with the good and the bad as a total package.

Dissatisfaction may sneak into the relationship as both of you have high expectations of each other and can be somewhat demanding. It's a good idea to foster respect by giving each other space and not judging too harshly. That would be the best foundation upon which this match can be built.

You may need to take things more slowly with Scorpios born between 24 October and 2 November because Mars and Pluto, which co-rule them, are really quite different to you. There could be a personality clash with these individuals and so they are not altogether suited for a long-term relationship with you.

Your connections with Scorpio natives born between 3 and 12 November are very well suited to you for love and marriage. Because Jupiter has a strong influence over them and is also the planet that primarily influences your marital affairs, this will be a natural fit. You'll feel a link of destiny between these characters.

With Scorpios born between 13 and 22 November, you'll be walking an emotional tightrope. Finances are also not exactly their forté. It's probably not a good idea to get involved with these people unless it's purely on a business basis. However, if you do choose to marry or spend long periods with them, make sure you both have clear guidelines for how you will deal with money issues.

VIRGO + SAGITTARIUS
Earth + Fire = Lava

Virgo has a reputation for being primarily concerned with detail, perfection and making sure that each piece of the jigsaw fits in place. Sagittarius has a very different approach to life and is a 'big picture person'. They will be happy to let Virgo put all the pieces of the jigsaw together as long as they can enjoy the final portrait.

Based upon this rather basic difference, we can assume that your relationship with Sagittarius will be poles apart. Yes, you are quite different and need to understand that your desire to investigate every nook and cranny will frustrate Sagittarius, who has a much freer and happy-go-lucky attitude.

The only way you will foster a positive relationship together is if you're able to accept Sagittarius and curb your natural tendency to find fault. This will require a considerable amount of trust on your part as they are concerned primarily with the outcome. Their plans may not always work out as you or they expect, but their view is that the outcome will be

VIRGO

worth it even if the journey is not particularly in keeping with the rules. This is a hard concept for you to get your head around.

You bring value to the relationship and, if they are open enough to see that your suggestions have merit and can improve the outcome, then the relationship will be all the better for it. Likewise, if you're able to imbibe the light-heartedness and free and easy attitude of Sagittarius, you'll enjoy your life so much more. So, the best case scenario is that a relationship with Sagittarius can positively enhance both your lives.

The way you love is poles apart from Sagittarius. Being more reserved you're not likely give away too much. In not expressing your emotions as openly as Sagittarius they may misinterpret this as disinterest or snobbery. They prefer an experimental approach to lovemaking, which gives vent to their fiery urges. You need to cast aside these differences and learn to overcome your fear of rejection. Don't analyse the relationship intellectually.

You'll enjoy relations with Sagittarians born between 23 November and 1 December. Individuals born throughout this period are probably the best suited to a relationship with you and their enterprising spirit will attract you. They are also natural travellers and love exploring the world and you are not averse to this, either.

You'll feel somewhat aggravated in a relationship with Sagittarians who are born between 2 and 11 December. Your arguments could even get overheated and cause you health problems in the long run. If you enter a relationship with them please make sure you control your reactions.

You're not particularly fulfilled with Sagittarians born between 12 and 22 December, either, but you should never judge a book by its cover because there are some aspects with these people that will also interest you and give you the chance to grow. They enjoy meeting people from different cultures.

VIRGO + CAPRICORN
Earth + Earth = Solid ground

Virgo and Capricorn may not be a match made in heaven but it can come close in the right circumstances. The combination of earth signs is astrologically well suited on many levels and is a great basis for a solid and enduring relationship.

Capricorn is an extremely ambitious sign and is well supported by you, Virgo. On the most practical level this is an excellent match that mutually serves both of you financially. It also works on an everyday level as well. You offer Capricorn clear insights into how they can achieve their grand goals. And they appreciate these hunches.

Capricorn will benefit from your up-beat and chirpy attitude because they tend to be somewhat serious about life. You have a refreshing approach that will make them feel a little less sombre.

You enjoy fine banter and provide Capricorn with a little more pleasure than what they are used to. Capricorn will slowly open up to your ways and can also make you feel extremely secure about your future. They are hard-working and know how important your material goals are to you.

It's not all business between Virgo and Capricorn, however. If you look a little more closely you'll see that romance and emotions seem to flow quite naturally between you. You can both be amorous with each because you feel an innate understanding together.

Capricorn is one of the few star signs that require less of your critical tongue lashings than other signs. You trust their integrity and know that they can do the job in the way you yourself would do it. They may take a little longer but you prefer a job well done. Because Capricorn won't feel browbeaten by you, they are more likely to open up and reveal the sensitive side of their personality, which is often not seen.

If you engage in a relationship with Capricorn born between 11 and 20 January you can expect a first-rate connection. They are particularly well suited to you because of the fact that Mercury co-rules them, which just happens to be your ruling planet as well. This is certainly a recipe for success in a love affair.

With Capricorns born between 23 December and 1 January you will also find a natural flow of energy between you. In particular, financial and material compatibility will work well as you trust them with your financial security. However, experiencing a better emotional and sexual relationship with them may take a little more time.

You are sexually and sensually enamoured by Capricorns born between 2 and 10 January because of the fact that Venus, the planet of love, dominates their personalities, along with Saturn. You can also expect a great social life with them that will eventually lead to a long-term, committed relationship.

VIRGO + AQUARIUS
Earth + Air = Dust

If you're looking for a word to sum up a relationship between Virgo and Aquarius go no further than 'challenging'.

Because Aquarius is related to your professional or work experiences, don't be surprised that you meet them through business circumstances or through a mutual co-worker or friend. As long as your arrangement is that of a professional nature, you may not experience the challenges that I initially indicate here. But once your romantic flames of passion have been sparked, you'll both enter a new phase.

STAR SIGN COMPATIBILITY

Just because you have much in common with Aquarius doesn't mean it will go that smoothly. Certainly, you will experience some similarities—for example, their desire for humanitarian and social improvement. This resonates with your sense of service. But there are some differences as well. They are concerned with the long-term ramifications of their revolutionary actions. You prefer to take things slowly and study each and every aspect of a project. Their noble ideas do, however, appeal to you and, even if it's not a romantic relationship, you can strike up a great friendship with them.

There is an idealistic connection between the two of you; perhaps this is karmic. In time the two of you will combine your powers perhaps to work for a greater cause. However, if you want this to succeed you mustn't superimpose your perfectionist attitudes on Aquarius or things could stall.

When all is said and done, Aquarius and their ideals don't fit in to your intellectual framework. We may also apply these principles to your sexual involvement together. It appears that part of your lesson with them is to become less reserved, more experimental and daring. Aquarius can be a great teacher to you; if only for the experience, you might like to give this relationship a go for a while.

Out of the group of Aquarians, the best match would be with those born between 31 January and 8 February. They have somewhat similar intellectual leanings and so your communication with them will be fulfilling. They generally have similar interests and this will also augment your partnership.

Aquarians born between 9 and 19 February are reasonably suitable for you and, if you're after a sexual affair, this could be the group that will satisfy you most. You'll feel less inhibited with them, which can mean an opportunity for you to develop your self-esteem.

With those born between 21 and 30 January, you can expect a more difficult relationship. Keep these people at arms length romantically but in a professional sense you will probably work well together. If you're already friends with them, it's probably best to keep it that way.

VIRGO + PISCES
Earth + Water = Mud

Because of their ability to love unconditionally, Pisces will make you may feel somewhat embarrassed when you first become involved with them. You will not feel as if you can love as freely and idealistically as them but it's only a matter of time until you will want to express your love in the same way. Some of the spiritual traits of Pisces are bound to rub off on you in due course. Pisces is a water sign and extremely loving. It is also the marriage sign for Virgo so there is a natural inclination to want to explore a relationship with them.

Pisces are the dreamers of the zodiac whereas Virgos are practical doers. The fact that Pisces lives in a realm of impractical ideas is difficult for you to reconcile, especially with your need to see tangible results. You will certainly experience love for Pisces but will also feel uncomfortable in their 'let's live in the moment' philosophy.

Both of your star signs are mutable, which means you're also changeable and moody by nature. You'll try to understand Pisces with your mind and they will try to intuit you with their emotions. This appears to be a relationship similar to parallel railway tracks travelling in the same direction but never quite coming together.

You have to be more than clever if you want to play the self-help game with Pisces by making suggestions as to how they can improve themselves. These are probably the most sensitive individuals you will meet so your observations and recommendations may be taken all too personally due to their thin-skinned nature. Please be careful in how you handle their emotions.

Your best combination is with Pisces born between 20 and 28 or 29 February. They can offer you a more stable life due to their grounded approach. You can develop a fulfilling relationship with them and learn all about your own feelings in the process.

If you involve yourself with a Pisces born between 1 and 10 March you will become great friends as they are sensitive admirers of yours. Actually, they secretly wish to have the same mental sharpness that you do, even if they don't articulate this fact. They will be great supporters of anything you choose to do in life.

You will experience good fortune and a great future with Pisces born between 11 and 20 March. The reason for this is that they have wonderful speaking skills and you respect this. They may not be as open to your criticisms, however, so do be careful to sweeten your opinions if you would like them to change in any way. They may be more retaliatory than you expect, so don't think they're going to take your criticisms lying down.

VIRGO

2009: The Year Ahead

VIRGO

A man of character finds a special attractiveness in difficulty, since it is only by coming to grips with difficulty that he can realise his potentialities.

—Charles de Gaulle

Romance and friendship

For you Virgo, your life has come full circle and it is now time for you to think seriously about a whole new level of expression in your relationships. The year 2009 will certainly weed out many of those aspects of your nature that have been holding you back in terms of enhancing your friendships, intimate relationships and marriage if you happen to be permanently committed.

Early in the year you will soon realise that social and family life are not simply to be based on fun. Fortunately, as a Virgo, your natural inclination is towards service anyway, but this year you will be much more sympathetic and attuned to the needs of those people in your life whom you consider important, special.

Due to this heightened sensitivity you will be keen to take practical measures to improve or fix what you see as defects in your relationships. Please be mindful of the fact, however, that even if you recognise character flaws in others and have explained this to them, it is not necessarily going to make them change their way. Now, this is the year, especially in the first part of 2009, when your example will be a guiding light for those you are trying to help.

Due to Mars and the Sun you will be much more energetic in January and February and will want to be heard. This is why I say that making a lot of noise won't necessarily achieve the results you are after in your personal life. If things don't go exactly the way you planned, you must not allow yourself to get crabby or resentful towards your partner.

There is opportunity to serve your loved ones in a unique way this year. Doing small, thoughtful favours by helping them in the less obvious parts of their lives, will be one way that you can certainly improve the quality of your love life this year. You will notice that by living up to the Virgo ideal of true, selfless service, you will be opening doors to those you love and helping them to aspire to the same sort of unconditional love that seems to be inherently a part of your nature.

You are extremely idealistic and imaginative about your love life this year. This is a year where finding your soulmate and perfect lover will be very high on your agenda and, if you are still on the lookout for that very special person, one piece of important advice I would like to give you at the outset is to be less serious, less pushy and less opinionated.

Due to Saturn continuing its movement in your sun sign of Virgo, throughout 2009 until November, the tendency to be emotionally brittle will work against you, so please lighten up and this will make the world of difference socially and sexually as well.

You will develop some very powerful relationships this year. I see you experiencing an incredible amount of passion but this can also make you highly emotional, particularly towards the end of February and early in March when Venus and Pluto move into a challenging aspect. If you haven't been in a relationship for sometime and you are suddenly infatuated by someone magnificent, please do be careful not to push them away before you even have the relationship off the ground.

In March and April, the Sun and Mars activate your desire for love and committed relationships. There is also a difficult stretch during the period of April to early May when Mars and Saturn can cause you and your partner a great deal of frustration. You must remain open to the fact that personalities change and indeed relationships are subject to these same forces of nature. You must avoid trying to keep things 'the way

VIRGO

they were'. The year 2009 will challenge you to grow and to adjust as you grow as a couple.

The action of Mars can cause some problems for you in relationships after May but more so in the area of your social peer group. You will enjoy most forms of recreation and other social activities and this will lift your self-image considerably. However, you must remember that being too forceful might antagonise some of your existing friends who are not able to handle the dramatic changes that they see all too quickly. Be gentle if you are trying to turn over a new leaf and to become a new person in a sense. People need time to adjust to these sorts of operations in your personality.

Travel is excellent throughout May and, if you sense that you have a busy schedule in other areas of your life at this time, I suggest you get away for a while and have a mid-year break. Your creative energies will also be strong throughout June and you can join forces with either friends or family members to make this a period of deep inner and spiritual fulfilment. This is a time when sharing will be more important than ever.

Keep working on your self-image throughout June. Consider your strong points and don't dwell on the past areas of your ways. Continue to foster only the best in yourself and this will have a wonderful effect on your social life, particularly in July when many new and engaging opportunities to mix with a new group of people arise. You will be able to express yourself freely and others will be fascinated by what you have to say.

In your closest relationships, there is every likelihood that this opening up will draw your lover closer to you. This may be hard at first because, of course, talking about the most private parts of yourself can make you somewhat vulnerable. But I don't see your loved ones using this against you; rather, it will reflect their need to do the same. This will therefore be a time when your passions as well as your intimate moments can be mutually very fulfilling.

Venus and Mars combining in the upper part of your horoscope throughout July and August, indicate that your zest for life will get stronger and stronger. You will be keen to explore different philosophical viewpoints and you will also challenge others to think along the same lines. This will continue in your relationship now. It may not last for long but will certainly be an eye opener and give you many memories that you can take into the future.

Responsibilities in your personal life weigh heavily upon you throughout September when the Sun and Saturn combine. I see this also impacting upon your personal freedom.

There is the possibility that, if you are a parent, this could simply mean adjusting your schedule to accommodate your children's needs. For Virgos who are new mums, it goes without saying, that this could be an extraordinarily challenging time in your life when your personal freedom and happiness will be constrained by the demands of your child or, if you have more than one, your 'sanity'. On that point, why not call upon family and friends to see if they can give you a hand? Why let your pride get in the road?

A dispute with a loved one in the later part of September could make this situation much worse than it needs to be. You are sensitively reacting to people's suggestions or desires to help you; as a result this might be a harder month than you expect. Accept people's advice graciously and don't feel obliged to act upon that advice.

October seems to offer you a little more in the way of self-satisfaction, with the combination of Venus and Mercury in the Sun sign. You can again feel more attractive to the world around you. I see this as an opportune month to shine your best light to the world around you.

You can again attract some interesting characters into your life, some of whom can become long-term friends.

VIRGO

In November and December, family matters take centre stage. An important transition takes place with Saturn moving to the sign of Libra. Most astrologers dispute that this second zone of your horoscope has anything to do with family, but this astrologer is quite adamant about the fact that Saturn's transit here will indeed create some changes to your family life or living circumstances.

The pressure may be on right into December to move house, to make some drastic changes; but of course, with Christmas looming, you don't want to overload yourself, even if the tendency is there to mix with as many people as you can. Wait till the mad December rush is over before committing yourself to any changes that could cause some upheaval to your family and friends in this last part of the year.

Communication is your forté and, with Mercury and Venus combining in the area of your domestic sphere, I see this as being your insurance against any serious problems or impulsive moves that can backfire.

Yes, 2009 is a special year in which your romantic ideals can be realised.

Work and money

This year you won't be waiting around for things to happen because Mars and Sun dominate your mental landscape, especially in the first part of 2009, and this indicates you will be zealously going after what you want.

Success is dependent upon energy, drive and purposeful action, backed by a good plan. In 2009 I see that all of these factors coming together to provide you with the perfect tools to achieve what you desire professionally and financially.

You will have to persevere through some of the challenges and the demands of your work due to the continued influence of Saturn in your work affairs. Luckily your drive and ambition is strong enough to counteract these setbacks. Even if you feel as if you are pushing a huge load uphill, you know in your heart of hearts that it is only temporary and that things are moving slowly but surely.

There is a certain eccentricity about your work practices during this cycle. Your sixth zone of work is particularly jam-packed with planets, especially in February and March where you must be careful that you don't spread yourself too thinly. You will be trying to play it safe, but at the same time will want quicker results. You will be walking a fine line between self-control and throwing everything you have got at your plan. You will have to make a decision and let the chips fall where they will.

You can achieve a tremendous amount in March, after which time the planets will begin to spread out and afford you some relief. You will then be able to focus more easily on individual aspects of your work, your profession and finances.

In April I see an exciting array of opportunities related to banking and earning money from such things as your superannuation. Any change you choose to make at this time might not be easy because you will be cautious and uncertain as to whether a move will pay better dividends; but I say this combination of planets is favourable and you should seriously consider a change for the better.

In May you'll be in two minds about work. You may wrestle with issues associated with co-workers and the calibre of professionalism that is being exhibited by those around you. To improve your skills it is always a better idea to work with people who are more experienced and capable of lifting you up to their standards rather than being with people who are lazy and not prepared to work to the same extent as you are.

These are serious issues that may be holding you back and, during the middle of the year, especially when the Sun comes to the career zone in June, a fantastic opportunity will

VIRGO

arise. Do your homework carefully before jumping ship or accepting a new offer of work. When Mercury re-enters your career zone and in particular at the end of June and early July, your decision-making processes will be much clearer and you will be happy with the choices you make.

Your finances take a turn for the better in the second half of the year, especially in late July and early August when your finance ruler Venus tracks through your career zone, and there's every likelihood your income can increase. This is also augmented by the fact that Venus activates your profit zone in August as well.

Creativity is going to be vitally important to you in September. If you find yourself in the public eye you will need to be the central figure of a work project or an engagement in public relations. Pay more attention to how you can present your case even if it seems a little flamboyant to you.

September is your month, when the Sun turns to its birth position and this indicates a growing confidence in your own abilities, which you will need due to the additional responsibilities that may be thrown your way. As I mentioned in your romantic forecast, this has to do with the combination of the Sun and Saturn. Saturn is actually quite a positive planet and endows you with sufficient discipline and concentration to get the work done. Whatever responsibilities you take on will be completed with the diligence and attention to detail that only Virgo can perform. I therefore predict a successful outcome.

A close friend or even your marriage partner might become closely involved in your work practices in some respect this year. They may not necessarily become part of the job, but their advice will be very useful to you in October and November.

In the closing month of the year, my last bit of advice is that you should be careful not to take on the problems of co-workers, who may be looking to you for more help than they deserve.

Balance your own personal needs and objectives with theirs. By doing so, 2009 will ultimately be a year in which you can say you achieve a heck of a lot.

Karma, luck and meditation

In January, February, May and June, your karma will be strong and you will need to be aware enough to take advantage of the opportunities that have been presented to you. Much of this will culminate in July with the conjunction of Venus and Mars in your zone of your past karma.

What this means is that the deeds you have performed in your life are likely to come full circle. Only you know whether your actions have been positive or not. If your intentions have been noble, something special can take place for you, Virgo, in the months of July, August and September. Otherwise, you'll need to put in extra time with paying some of your karmic debts.

If you are not familiar with this concept, it is a very simple one. Life is simply an accountant's balance sheet: debits and credits. If you have clocked up debits then, just like a bank loan, you need to cough up the money. Fortunately, I don't see a problem for most Virgos. Your karma is usually quite good and your intentions are transparent. Good for you. This will help to bring you success in your work, relationships and family.

Another important part of the year is September. This is a meditative month in which you can take time off to reconnect with the deeper parts of your character and spiritual self. You will benefit from by this, and in turn your family and friends will also benefit from some of the positive repercussions.

Love and romance is favoured when Venus and Mercury combine in October. Family life will be a source of great happiness to you in December, so share as much of the love and good fortune with whomever you can, especially during the festive season.

Good luck, Virgo!

VIRGO

2009:
Month by Month
Predictions

JANUARY

Twenty years from now you will be more disappointed by the things you didn't do than by the ones you did. So throw off the bowlines, sail away from the safe harbor. Catch the trade winds in your sails. Explore. Dream.

—Mark Twain

Highlights of the month

This is an ideal month for dedicating yourself to your career objectives, and for those of you who are looking for new work, this is a very lucky cycle. If you do happen to be employed already, however, make the most of your skills and don't be afraid to show just what you can do. Your intention and planning will make an impression on others and you should use this energy up until the 5th to achieve as much as you can.

Increased responsibilities needn't be a downer. For some Virgos the movement of Saturn across the Sun sign position could bring additional pressures and challenges on both career and the home front. You may be working extra long hours to achieve deadlines or to play catch-up with your bills or other debt.

If you're not enjoying the work you're doing it's not a bad idea to consider a new line of work, but remember the old saying 'There's no point jumping out of the frying pan into the fire' because the grass is not always greener on the other side.

While the Sun is transiting your zone of creativity and love affairs, you'll be really inspired to make the most of this time away from your professional activities. Believe it or not, even though I see considerable pressures hanging over your head, it's not the time to be discouraged or put yourself down. Rather, I see you switching off and making the most of your social activities. Such things as the performing arts, sports or similar events will really appeal to you in a way that can be excellent counterbalances to these other issues.

Your romantic vibes are strong this month and this is due to Mars also activating the zone of love affairs. A relationship of some sort is likely to start or at least get hotter during this period.

A shift in values is also earmarked for you throughout January, and whatever it is you hold dear in terms of belief systems can indeed be totally eliminated in favour of some new idea or attitude. Around the 25th, try to tone it down if you're in the company of others who aren't quite as progressive in their thinking as you are.

Between the 19th and 23rd, a sharing of some success, perhaps your partner's or a friend's accomplishments, will be a cause for celebration. By sheer association you'll be able to enjoy the benefits of this success as well.

In the last few days of the month your vitality and self-esteem will reach a great height due to the influence of Mars and the Sun. Make sure you have ample physical activities to let off some of this powerful steam.

Romance and friendship

With Saturn easing up on your relationships, you'll feel much more light-hearted in your closest relationships around the

VIRGO

1st. Great communication is also promised due to Mercury and Jupiter providing you some fun times with the one you love.

When Venus enters your marital zone on the 3rd, passions can run hot and you are likely to feel amorous and very sensual. This could be a deciding moment in taking your relationship to the next level.

On the 5th you could feel extremely intense with someone's behaviour. They may retaliate and misinterpret your good intentions. Be gentle on lovers and friends today.

Communications can move into a tailspin around the 12th. You must be clear and concise in conveying your messages because Mercury's retrograded movement is notorious for withholding facts and causing misunderstandings.

Between the 12th and the 20th you'll be running on all eight cylinders, but be careful not to drive yourself into the ground. Numerous calls, associations and possibly even parties, will drain you of your valuable energy. It may be fun but by the 20th you'll be feeling as if you need a good rest.

Around the 23rd Venus and Uranus provide you with an unexpected and exciting chance meeting. Remember how your heart used to flutter when you thought you'd met the person of your dreams? This could be one of those moments.

The 24th, 25th and 26th are important dates for re-establishing the terms of your relationships with others. Set aside time for important discussions if you feel things have slipped a little off track. By the 27th, when Mercury and Venus enter a good relationship, you can clarify any misunderstandings. The 31st is wonderful for reigniting the flame of love and you're likely to feel highly fulfilled by the gestures of someone close to you.

Work and money

There's a strong work ethic dominating your actions throughout the period of the 3rd to the 6th. When Jupiter enters your zone of work and daily routine, you can expect some promising results. A new opportunity or a breakthrough in your workplace relations can be expected.

You can shine a light on employment matters on the 12th when the Sun creates a dazzling aura around you. You'll be quick and correct in your evaluation of some of the issues at hand. This will win you considerable respect around the 19th. You can expect some sort of mini-promotion around the 21st.

A solar eclipse takes place on the 26th and this highlights the need for you to eliminate some of the excess baggage that is holding you back from reaching your true potential. You'll have some deep insights that will help pave the way for greater successes at this time.

You could be out of step with your workmates around the 29th when a fashion statement or attitude that you portray doesn't sit well with them. Don't push your barrow too hard and by the 31st a resolution can take place.

Destiny dates

Positive: 1, 3, 4, 6, 21, 23, 24, 26, 31

Negative: 29

Mixed: 5, 12, 13, 14, 15, 16, 17, 18, 19, 20, 25

FEBRUARY

Highlights of the month

Some important decisions may need to be made throughout February and between the 1st and 5th your mind will be mulling over paperwork and previous discussions you might have had. I see you deep in thought and communication in presenting your side of things.

You can't please everyone all of the time so between the 4th and 11th you may have to make an unpleasant choice between spending time with loved ones and committing yourself to additional work demands. You won't necessarily want to stir up trouble so it could be a case of keeping things close to your chest, which will blow up when you reveal what you have in mind.

Between the 8th and 11th your finances are in a good state and you'll have the benefits of someone else's expertise and experience to help you through any of your financial questions.

On the 5th till the 8th you may be quarrelsome and your patience may be tested, but try not to lose your cool and take out your irritable moments on those who are only trying to help you. You have the opportunity to act as a leader, to help others through your own example, between the 6th and 10th. You'll be all fired up in your work and will probably be moving

2009: FEBRUARY

just a bit too quickly for others who may start to become competitive. Try to be more of a team player throughout this cycle.

Between the 13th and 18th there'll be ample opportunity for you to improve your knowledge base and somehow enhance your skills or even your working conditions. You can extend this to your personal life as well, which will mean learning new techniques for expressing yourself and bringing out the best in your partner.

By the 17th, the Sun will move to your important partnership, marriage and public relations zone, which will spotlight these areas of your life. You'll have to sacrifice some of your own personal interests so you can meet the needs of your important 'other'. This will actually work in your favour and bring you considerable happiness if you're prepared to go with the flow.

Uranus the planet of revolution and change is challenging you to break free of some of your responsibilities and your personal interests. You'll be tempted to buck the system, which is something quite out of character, especially in the last part of the month.

In the last few days of the month, try to be a little more open-minded with others who present you with a story that doesn't seem credible. Until you know all the facts, suspend your judgement because you might be able to learn something from the experience.

Romance and friendship

Any lack of clarity in your communications with friends will be cleared up when Mercury moves in forward motion on the 1st. If you've been waiting to make a decision or give someone the all clear, you can do so right now and feel confident about the outcome.

VIRGO

Some wonderful news can arrive around the 2nd and this can lift your confidence and self-esteem in a friendship.

Between the 3rd and 6th your sexual appetite will be on the increase due to Venus's occupation of your zone of sexuality and deeper emotions. This is a perfect time to raise that level of intimacy and get closer to the one you love.

On the 6th, 14th and also the 18th, you need to be careful not to be excessive in your lifestyle choices. This is a period when you may overdo it—drinking, eating, partying and generally having a good time. Remember, what goes up, must come down.

The wonderful aspect between Venus and Mars on the 18th has all the hallmarks of a passionate office affair. Knowing your personality type, you're likely to want to keep this a secret if it does happen. You know the old saying: 'Business and pleasure don't mix.'

Monitor your spouse or partner's financial habits, particularly between the 18th and 23rd. You may have some disagreements over financial issues but I can assure you that this is just the tip of the iceberg and reflecting some deeper dissatisfaction between you.

The month finishes on an electric note with Mercury, Venus, Uranus and the Sun all creating a rather abrupt set of circumstances where you'll have to take off at a moment's notice. The excitement will be enticing but the aftermath will be additional work that will leave you feeling a little regretful, but not altogether disappointed.

Work and money

Contractual arrangements can be finalised on the 1st and this will result in a win–win situation for all concerned.

A smoother, more balanced form of communication on the 2nd can win over a client or two and put you ahead of the rest, especially if you happen to be in communications or sales.

Finances are high on your agenda on the 3rd, with Venus activating your banking, insurance and investment activities. Growing your nest egg will seem more important than ever just now.

Between the 5th and the 9th you'll be balancing tried and tested methods that have worked for you against some progressive and technological systems. This may not sit easily with you but persist with it because the results will shortcut your path to success.

The lunar eclipse on the 10th indicates you may need to spend a little more time in a close-knit and undistracted environment to achieve a lot more. Others may think you're shrugging them off but it is essential to stay on track to achieve the sort of results you're destined for this year.

You can make a big impact upon others after the 18th, with your words carrying much more weight than even you had given yourself credit for. By the 26th that letter of recommendation or an acceptance on some new job will arrive and make you feel very happy, indeed.

Destiny dates

Positive: 1, 2, 3, 8, 9, 10, 11, 13, 15, 16, 17, 26

Negative: 19, 20

Mixed: 4, 5, 6, 7, 14, 18

MARCH

Highlights of the month

If you've met your personal responsibilities this month, there shouldn't be too much of a problem; but if you've been avoiding them, or simply ignoring your partner's needs, this could be a difficult month. Between the 2nd and 4th, miscommunications aggravate the situation so be careful to make sure your e-mails or other correspondences are double-checked before sending them off. Other people could also be communicating in ways that are confusing and apt to create differences.

This is a month where your physical vitality is strong but you are also impulsive and likely to be in a hurry. From the 5th to the 9th take extra precautions by allowing more time to get to your destination in a casual manner. Take care of your body if you are exercising and don't overdo it.

The movement of Mercury to your marital zone after the 8th reflects your need to seek good advice. You'll be surprised that talking with someone during this cycle will be very helpful and can lead you to understand many new topics and subjects as a result.

Competition after the 13th is strong both from you and others. You may find yourself in a position of rivalry with someone you least expect. If you choose to enter a relationship now, you should brace yourself for a period, as the person will be hard to please and also just as competitive as yourself. Try to play it cool and under no circumstances get drawn into games of betterment.

Between the 16th and the 22nd you'll be very self-absorbed and will want to carve out an independent path for yourself. If you've been feeling controlled at work or smothered in any relationship, you'll be desperately trying to find some way to break free of the situation. If you feel angry with someone, it's best to put pen to paper and send them a note rather than confronting them face to face.

Between the 19th and 25th you have a strong desire to reach a deeper level of intimacy with your spouse or partner. As well, if there have been issues bothering you from the past, this is the time to talk about it and clear the air.

Romance and friendship

On the 4th you'll be full of enthusiasm and will want to share your excitement with friends. Try not to wear rose-coloured glasses, however, because you'll overlook the fact that others may not be as enthusiastic as yourself. On the 5th keep your expectations realistic and don't be too airy-fairy when trying to share your enthusiasm with friends.

Between the 7th and the 10th, your relationships might appear to be going backwards quickly. Fill in the details of your biggest plan, the bigger picture of your love life rather than bogging down in the nitty-gritty details.

On the 11th, you might feel a little let down by someone's opinion of you. They may be brutally honest and your sensitivity might react to what they have to say. Be creative in your responses.

Mars enters your seventh house of relationships on the 15th so this means your loved ones are less likely to want to

VIRGO

compromise and will not see things your way. I see this as a period of tension if you let it get under your skin.

Between the 17th and the 21st you may find that your career objectives are at odds with what your friends or lover expect of you. You may have to justify your actions and this could be both confusing and frustrating.

I see you gaining considerable assistance through a friend around the 22nd. This will come as a welcome relief if you're feeling frustrated with some personal issue in your life. It's nice to know you still have good friends.

Some of the obligations you have just now may feel a bit overwhelming, so between the 28th and the 31st try to stick to your guns and reward yourself once the task is completed.

Work and money

When Mars and Neptune are associated the surrounding atmosphere can be both devitalising and also confusing, especially in work matters. Around the 8th you'll feel as if your actions are not appreciated and that the focus of others is blurred. Re-establish what you expect to achieve through the work you're doing and, if you feel unfulfilled, change the game plan.

For independently employed Virgos, the 9th to the 15th is an important period in which negotiations and partnerships are high on the agenda. Beginning a new business with someone who is able to help you achieve financial security is likely now, but please do take care around the 9th, 12th and then again on the 16th, when discussions get bogged down in differences. Having a mediator present is always a good idea under these transits.

Your visions can again be much clearer by the 23rd when Neptune provides you with ample creative ammunition to develop something fresh and inspiring for yourself and others. You could now achieve a short-term goal.

2009: MARCH

Don't push your business case too hard between the 27th and 31st. Ask questions and, better still, give others a chance to respond, even if it's not in the time frame you would prefer.

Destiny dates

Positive: 12, 14, 16, 22, 23, 24, 25

Negative: 5, 6

Mixed: 2, 4, 7, 8, 9, 10, 11, 13, 15, 17, 18, 19, 21, 27, 28, 29, 30, 31

APRIL

Highlights of the month

A desire arises in you this month to express the best part of your character to your mate or loved one. You want to create a safe haven for yourself and family and will be fostering co-operation in all your relationships.

In fact, you'll be so good natured that others are likely to take advantage of you. By all means help people where you can but you mustn't become a pushover.

This month, Mars and Saturn enter into a complicated tussle and this can cause you some irritation, frustration and delays, especially if you are expecting a breakthrough in your professional life. The doors are open but unforeseen obstacles and glitches may make the dreams that you cherish a little harder to make real just now.

Amid these challenges there is support and your creative ideas can take off, particularly around the 8th when you seek a new group of friends or career path that can give you greater assistance in attaining your ambitions. For the time being you may also wish to put some of your passionate desires on hold but I don't see that lasting for long as Mars continues to stimulate your relationships for just a little while longer.

Journeys are well favoured, especially after the 15th. Exposing yourself to different cultures and new geographical interests will be high on your agenda. The new Moon on the 25th, along with Mercury's transit in your zone of long-distance travels, is the cause of this.

Try to develop closer relationships and a greater degree of understanding with your siblings and neighbours after the 21st. In the last week of the month, disputes are likely and this can be anything from an outstanding loan to business dealings that may be afoot. Disputes over land and territory are also other areas to which Mars can direct its ferocious vibrations. Personal power and issues of control dominate.

Your finances do well from the 26th onwards. Money and social lives seem to be intertwined as friends offer you their assistance in some venture or moneymaking scheme. Your relationships improve on a much deeper level than you had previously experienced. I see many opportunities for you to enjoy your relationships on the most intimate and sexual level thanks to Venus.

On the 30th, your career is highlighted, big time. Mercury moves into the upper part of the heavens and signifies that work projects and relationships you have with others in the workplace will be very satisfying. Your aspirations will reach a peak.

Romance and friendship

Are you demanding love or simply facilitating the expression of warmth and affection from your friends and loved ones around the 4th? If you demand love, you may simply push people away and that seems to be the lesson for the first week or so of April. A very tough aspect between Mars and Saturn takes place on the 5th and this requires a delicate balancing act on your part. You may clearly feel that someone is not showing you the love that you feel you deserve, but your pride will not allow you to ask 'those' questions.

VIRGO

Good aspects are forming for you between the 7th and 12th. Mercury and Venus can show you the way. You'll realise that your spouse or partner is worth the effort at this time and you'll be prepared to make some additional concessions because of this.

Take care of your health between the 12th and the 16th. If you belong to a gym or sporting club, and you're trying to impress someone you feel attracted to, you may push yourself beyond reasonable limits and cause some injury. Now, the result will not only be unimpressive, but a little embarrassing, too.

Venus moves into forward motion on the 18th and this is an excellent moment for you to feel confident that the problems of your love life are now behind you.

The new Moon on the 25th has a strong flavour of travel, culture and higher education and this can be blended with your social interests up until the 28th when friendships reach a peak again.

Laying low between the 29th and the 30th will be an excellent spiritual tonic for you and a time when you can quietly while away the odd hour or two with one of your best friends.

Work and money

Pluto is spurring you on to be daring, bold and maybe even a little speculative, especially around the 4th. Have you ever considered taking a gamble on life, on work and your professional direction? This may or may not relate to throwing money at the stock market or types of speculative business ventures, or in your case it could have to do with taking a gamble on your dreams.

Information you receive between the 5th and the 10th will motivate you to take a punt and move outside your professional comfort zone. This may be triggered by the hard aspects of Mars and Saturn. I suggest that you research, investigate and rethink everything through carefully and not act simply on an impulse or through dissatisfaction. All speculation should be done through well-informed judgement. You won't go wrong if you stick to this rule.

Some of your most positive achievements this month take place on the 15th, 23rd and again on the 25th, when the planets bring you several new opportunities to further your professional activities. Your income should see a marked improvement due to some of the above mentioned opportunities.

Destiny dates

Positive: 5, 6, 7, 8, 9, 10, 11, 18, 23, 25, 26, 27, 28, 29, 30

Negative: 13, 14, 16, 21

Mixed: 4, 12, 15

MAY

Highlights of the month

With the influence of Venus and Mars in your horoscope, this is a month when your sexual appeal is on a high. Between the 1st and 4th you'll appreciate your powers of persuasion much more. As a Virgo you probably don't consider yourself as appealing as really you are but the world will notice you and that's what counts!

Along with your natural, attractive appeal, the full Moon of the 9th accentuates your capacity to communicate very clearly and concisely. What you have to say will make a strong impression on others.

With Jupiter and Neptune in very close proximity in your work zone, particularly after the 15th, your work ideals will be either inspired or completely whacko—that's what others will think, anyway. Please be careful not to express your ideas too quickly until you've had a chance to test the water with others.

Networking with others after the 18th will help you reach the finishing line in record time. The benefits you receive now will want to be shared with everyone around you. There's a strong sense of co-operation and it's an excellent period for realising your full potential, both as an individual and with the group.

There's a period between the 19th and 21st when you might feel a little out-of-sorts with yourself and the environment around you, which is why by the 28th you may want to take some time-out, unwind and re-evaluate your position in the scheme of things. There could be tension associated with your relationships and this also has to do with the relationship between Mercury and Saturn. Slow and deliberate thinking will remedy this.

When the Sun strengthens its position in your career sector in the last week of the month, you'll be surprised at your personal and professional prowess. The new Moon of the 24th indicates a fresh approach to your professional activities and you will feel extremely confident that your ideas and your professional direction are taking shape. You'll be recognised for your hard work and it will be time for that promotion or pay rise.

Temptation is in the air between the 27th and 29th. You will find yourself in the company of people who are braver than you and prepared to do things you wouldn't ordinarily attempt. The excitement might be just too hard to resist, but think of the consequences and ensure that you don't indulge yourself to the extent that joining in compromises your integrity.

Romance and friendship

The first few days of May are not altogether as exciting as you'd like but there will be some comfort in the fact that the Sun and Saturn are a stabilising influence for you, particularly leading up to the 5th. Romantic and personal or domestic matters can run smoothly and you needn't expect too many dramas at this point.

On the 7th Mercury again turns retrograde and, although this influences your professional life more acutely, it does also tend to have a marked influence on your family affairs. Changes you expected to run smoothly—for example, moving

VIRGO

house, purchasing new items or luxury goods for your home—will not turn out as expected. This is simply a delay, so don't let your mind dwell on this.

Sometime around the 16th the health of your mother or a woman on the maternal side of your family may have some problems that can be a little harrowing. Again, do what you can but you mustn't let this interfere with the smooth functioning of your day-to-day life.

Between the 16th and 22nd, the influences of the Sun and Uranus on your marital and sexual affairs are sudden, exciting and unexpected. If you're invited to a party, get ready to be swept off your feet. If you're not able to meet the challenge, you'll regret not being a little more bold and dynamic.

By the 21st you'll be surprised when you realise that your way of thinking is very much attuned to some of the people to whom I have just referred. It's as if a part of your character that has been locked away for so long will spring to the surface and this will afford you the opportunity to develop your creativity.

Mercury goes direct on the 31st of May and this could indicate the arrival of something that has been delayed or finding something that has been mislaid.

Work and money

Both the new Moon and the retrograde Mercury occurring in your career zone testify to the fact that both your emotional and intellectual attention will primarily be on work-related issues this month.

You may be asked to consent to some course of action professionally around the 2nd, but I advise you to ask for an extended period of time in which to make your decision. Don't sign documents that are not absolutely clear and check the fine print. If necessary take the documents home and wait until the end of the month when Mercury goes direct.

2009: MAY

Some of your ethical and moral standards are challenged after the 13th. You may have to do someone else's dirty work and unfortunately you'll be between a rock and a hard place sorting out this matter. This is a hard one and I can't really advise you on that except to say that you may just have to take it as it comes.

The new Moon on the 24th up till the direct motion of Mercury on the 29th is an excellent time when you can give the thumbs up to anyone waiting on a decision from you. This could be the start of a whole new cycle in your work.

Destiny dates

Positive: 1, 3, 4, 5, 17, 18, 22, 24, 25, 26, 31

Negative: 13

Mixed: 2, 7, 16, 19, 20, 21, 27, 28, 29

JUNE

Highlights of the month

This is not a month to hold back in your romantic gestures. A magnanimous or even courageous gesture is necessary to move a relationship forward. The continuing association of Venus and Mars over the coming months hints at an ever-increasing satisfaction in your relationships. Go for it. The period of the 4th to the 7th is particularly notable in this respect.

You may not feel particularly settled if you're in a committed long-term relationship during this cycle and in fact some abrupt changes or at least recklessness characterises this period. Remain flexible and accept the situation by trying to feel appreciative for what you have rather than what is lacking. This is an important secret that many people overlook and is the continuing cause for unhappiness in their lives.

This month Venus accentuates your need for higher learning, philosophical insights and the general expansion of your mental horizons. Particularly by the 15th you'll be finding yourself in the company of like-minded people who have much to offer in the way of culture, intellectual stimulation and, if you resonate emotionally with them, the possibility for a relationship as well.

The Sun is in an excellent position to give you a lot of success, but men in authority in particular can be annoying when they try to obstruct you through jealousy or simply just wanting to be difficult. You need to pull out your best diplomatic weapons to overcome this hurdle.

When the Sun shifts its focus from work to social activities on the 20th, you'll be all fired up to look your best and attend social gatherings, club events and the odd soirée with friends. If you've had a desire to be part of a community group or charitable organisation, you could now put your best foot forward and investigate this more seriously.

Social pleasures and personal enjoyment seem to be even more emphasised from the 25th to the 28th and you'll feel yourself easing off in your rush to get things done and make an impact professionally. Friends will be the focus during the last few days of the month.

Around the 30th you'll find your health and vitality peaking. Jupiter ensures that if you've had any health problems these can be resolved quite easily and that your wellbeing will be back on track.

Romance and friendship

After the 1st you may have trouble keeping up with a friend's physical or mental appetites. You may want to cruise whereas your friend may want to travel and experience a lot more. The first few days of the month require a great deal of compromise on your part.

A drive for relationships on the 4th could be perceived by others to be a little relentless. Stop, look and listen to the impact you're having on people around you. This could be one of the factors that is impacting on what you are lacking romantically as well. Think on that.

Excellent romantic omens do occur after the 5th when Venus moves into the ninth zone of luck. An opportunity to

VIRGO

travel and engage with others at a distance is quite likely. You'll develop a love of culture, reading and even philosophy.

There's a form of eastern philosophy called Tantra, which talks about the spiritual meaning of relationships, and you may develop a taste for this topic and try to apply some of the principles to your own relationship.

If your spouse or closest friend demands some free time after the 15th, be gracious and try to understand this is no reflection on you or on the relationship as they may just be re-evaluating their own goals.

The Sun enters an excellent phase for socialising and rejuvenating your nearest and dearest friendships on the 21st. Here's your chance to re-cement the bonds of friendships and express how you feel for those you consider your best mates.

Between the 22nd and 28th I note a more active club life with music, bands and other theatrical performances likely to take centre stage in your life (excuse the pun).

If you're tired on the 30th, postpone that conversation until the following day to avoid any arguments. You need much more rest at this time, too.

Work and money

During June, you may endeavour to create a more aesthetic and artistic character to the work that you do. Around the 3rd this could be a pleasant challenge, especially if you're working in a dry, mathematical or practical field. Try to remain focused and above all love the work you do.

For a few days between the 6th and 10th there is an additional burden placed upon your shoulders. This is due to the aspect of the Sun and Saturn. A senior manager or someone who shares the load with you at work may not be available and the overflow of work may fall into your in-tray for a few days. You'll find yourself handling the extra round of work comfortably.

Your profitability, which I would say is a pay rise, is very likely after the 22nd. Is this because you handled the additional responsibilities so well? Perhaps. Maybe you've been expecting this for sometime, anyway.

You may be stuck with a problem that bothers you between the 26th and 30th. If you find this is an intellectual issue or one which your skills are not capable of dealing with, let go of your ego and ask for help.

Destiny dates

Positive: 3, 5, 20, 21, 22, 23, 24, 25, 30

Negative: 1, 8, 9, 10

Mixed: 4, 6, 7, 15, 26, 27, 28, 29

JULY

Highlights of the month

This is an important month for re-establishing your connections with people who somehow slipped through the cracks, disappeared from view and who have been a part of your life in the past but are no longer quite as present. You'll be reminiscing about old times, old friends and wondering where everyone is.

If you're missing a sibling or relative who's travelled somewhere or who has permanently left your locality, there may be good news around the 3rd, which brings them back into your life. There could be unfinished business that you need to work through with them.

The full Moon on the 7th is a wonderful omen that brings with it positive and confident vibrations, especially where workplace relationships may be concerned. New professional and social contacts can be looked forward to in this time frame.

Take some additional precautions with your health between the 8th and 13th. You need to be conscious of the fact that you may have an intolerance to some foods or possibly even environments in which you are spending a lot of time and this could be the cause of your fuzzy head or generally low level of energy. Systematically study your diet and observe how this is affecting your moods and your physical state.

Mars in the most prominent part of your horoscope throughout July affects you in terms of following your dreams and making a break from a situation in which you are uncomfortable. This may relate to a relationship as well as a job situation. If you've suppressed your feelings or have been threatened by someone else's larger ego, this could be an explosive period so you must try to manage your temper so that you don't say or do things you'll later regret.

Take care between the 15th and 20th because this is the time when these feelings may emerge very strongly. There could also be issues associated with contracts and workplace agreements and, if you've felt uncomfortable about some of the terms under which you've been working, you mustn't let your fear hold you back from negotiating a better set of conditions.

It's not a bad idea to wait until the 22nd when the new Moon gives you a fresh lease of life and the ability to wangle a good deal for yourself with a bit of cash as the pot of gold at the end of the rainbow.

Finances are also on the up after the 26th, which gives you the opportunity to purchase that item for the home that may have been in the back of your mind for sometime.

Romance and friendship

Throughout the middle part of the year, the conjunction of Venus and Mars is very telling on your romantic affairs and will bring quite a few prospective lovers out of the woodwork. Between the 1st and 4th I see that your energy levels are up to the task. Use this time to explore the mental as well as physical aspects and you will definitely learn a lot about human nature and how relationships work (and don't work).

VIRGO

On the full Moon of the 7th, 11th and again on the 15th and 16th, these patterns and planetary harbingers of good luck present their best opportunities to you. Please note that you may be tempted to act upon your impulses against your better judgement and this is not advisable. Rely on the advice of a close confidante.

Apart from any existing friends, a new friendship is likely to start around the 22nd. When you meet this person you'll feel a very close bond and a deeper understanding with them. Because the water sign of Cancer dominates your zone of friendships, the person may indeed be a Scorpio, Pisces or Cancerian. This will become a fruitful friendship and is likely to last for many years.

You may feel a little down around the 24th and 25th when the Moon transits Saturn and influences your relationships. You may be expecting more than your partner is able to give so don't be so demanding and let them lead you in terms of what they're capable of sharing with you.

Venus produces many aspects on the 25th, 27th, 28th and 29th. You could be getting mixed messages from a friend and this could leave you up in the air. If you ask the advice of a third party, this may also complicate matters. Wait until after the 30th to broach the topic or you could be in for a head-on confrontation.

Work and money

Education is high on your agenda, particularly in the first five or six days of the month. Up until the 6th, as dull as it may seem, accept an invitation to attend a lecture or listen to some keynote speakers who can throw some new light on the work you do.

You may be trying to do things bigger and better than everyone else between the 8th and 15th. Don't push too hard because as the old saying goes 'It's far superior to work smart than to work hard'. You may have a lot on your plate this month and could be trying to beat the deadlines but watch the stress levels. Slow and steady wins the race, so just take your time and enjoy your work.

Mars dominates your professional landscape after the 12th and this reinvigorates your career. You'll feel as if you've been injected with a dose of high-powered atomic energy. Nothing will stop you now, particularly around the 18th when your speed and agility will be most noticeable to others.

Virgos who are actively involved in sport as a career will find that the 20th to the 26th is extremely good for competitive wins and extra income.

Destiny dates

Positive: 1, 2, 3, 4, 7, 21, 22, 23, 26

Negative: 17, 19, 20

Mixed: 6, 8, 9, 10, 11, 12, 13, 14, 15, 16, 18, 24, 25, 27, 28, 29

AUGUST

Highlights of the month

You may have a very clear set of ideas on how you want to get things done this month. Your good judgement and clear thinking are notable and this is usually a part of your Virgo nature. However, others may not be quite as focused on the objective you have marked out and so a conflict of interests is likely.

Matters in your domestic situation are strongly in focus throughout August and may be serious enough to distract you from your own personal and social affairs for a while. After the 2nd, when Venus enters your social zone, you'll be torn between several social engagements and responsibilities with family members, possibly older relatives.

By the 20th you'll realise that, even if you've stalled and postponed meeting these obligations, you won't be able to sweep them under the rug any longer. From the 20th to the 24th should be a busy period but in a low-key way, behind the scenes, dealing with the nitty-gritty of these specific issues.

By the 27th you'll find that many of these issues can be resolved and, in fact, with the air clear and fresh again, you should be feeling pretty peaceful within yourself. An additional positive energy is the Sun returning to your birth sign, which will be a welcome relief from the dark shades of grey that may dominate the earlier part of August. You can feel revitalised from around the 22nd and get on with living life on your terms once again.

Competitive sports or at least an invitation to a game or match is likely after the 24th and gives you the chance to express yourself in a boisterous way with others. You mustn't hold back from screaming and shaking, rattling and rolling a little. This will be good therapy just now and will create an even more peaceful mental state in the last few days of the month.

With Mercury's entry into your zone of finances between the 24th and the 30th, you'll be much more attentive to your finances and any commercial transactions that are on the table. You'll be going through these matters with a fine-tooth comb to give yourself the assurance that your material security is well looked after. You can expect many discussions with your partner on how to spend and manage your money. Consulting with a good financial planner or accountant would be a good idea. This is a month in which you can start to reorder your financial affairs for the better.

Romance and friendship

Around the 2nd a friend returns, and this could be literally or figuratively speaking. If a mate has been travelling or residing in a foreign place and returns home, you can expect a celebration.

You'll need to take care of issues at home this month because the Moon shows you're emotionally tethered to some domestic issues and this could be more of a nuisance value than anything else. There's no escaping the fact that you'll have to deal with a loved one or a child between the 2nd and 8th. Your mind will be deeply absorbed in it and this can affect the quality of your other activities, if you let it overpower you.

VIRGO

Take care between the 11th and 14th. Mars in its hard aspect to Saturn will also cause difficulties and frustrations for you, not to mention danger or injury, so try not to rush about and take on too much. Around the 14th especially, you mustn't say 'yes' to a request if you know this is going to be difficult to fulfil. Be honest with your friends and tell them if you can't meet their desires.

You're overly generous between the 15th and 18th and giving more of your time than you have available or spending too much on a gift when your budget won't accommodate it. Everyone will love you for your magnanimous attitude, but you'll be quietly begrudging the fact.

The Sun and Mercury spend sometime in your quiet zone and, with the new Moon on the 20th also occurring there, this is again a spiritual phase that allows you to reconnect with the heart of your own personality. Helping others who are less fortunate than yourself is an excellent means of developing your spiritual and karmic potential. As I said, in the last few days of the month, don't overdo it and if you can't keep up, simply postpone to another day.

Work and money

Your dynamic drive continues throughout the month of August with Mars helping you achieve a tremendous amount in a very short space of time.

With Venus entering your zone of professional profits, the period from the 2nd up until the 9th in particular is auspicious for bolstering your profitability and the bottom line of your own company if you happen to run a business. Those employed should ask for that pay rise now and, with Venus's charming vibrations in support of this request, how could anyone refuse? Even if your boss is a little grouchy, won't you have a smirk on your face when you hear the words: 'Yeah, sure. How much do you want?'

2009: AUGUST

Between the 9th and 15th your vision for the new position is also likely to materialise. You mustn't let frustrations gnaw away at your inner peace. If you're in a dead-end job you'll be feeling the impact of that between the 11th and the 15th. This is a good time to take a leave of absence or time off without pay. It will be well worth it.

Excellent dates for getting a lot of work done are the 19th, 20th, 23rd and 26th. Between the 26th and 31st, your work and social life overlap with good results as well.

Destiny dates

Positive: 9, 19, 25, 26, 27, 28, 29, 30, 31

Negative: 11, 12, 13, 14

Mixed: 2, 3, 4, 5, 6, 7, 8, 15, 16, 17, 18, 20, 23, 24

SEPTEMBER

Highlights of the month

Your power of faith is extraordinary and during September you must rely on your inner resources to help you cope with the mounting load of work and responsibilities that I foresee. Between the 3rd and the 8th, you must act upon your beliefs without imposing your opinions on others. Your actions will speak much louder than words.

If you are in a close relationship, try to remind each other of the good feelings you share and the initial spark of passion that brought you together. Think back on your past and remember the good times, rather than pointing out each other's faults. This is the supreme remedy for any of your love ailments in September. Between the 14th and 19th I would even go so far as to say that you could spend some valuable time in a secluded environment with your loved one.

Singles should also attempt to get away for a while, as your karma to meet someone in an unusual place is strong.

The new Moon on the 18th tells me that you're due for a makeover—not so much a cosmetic one as an inner transformation—which will be visible on the outside for everyone to see.

2009: SEPTEMBER

You're turning over a new leaf this month, Virgo, and, while resolutions are normally saved for the new year, you might just choose to step forward a little bit earlier to bring forth your new personality.

This is not to say that you won't change aspects of your physical being and this can be done through simple measures such as a manicure, a day spa or even the purchase of some new and exciting fashion.

Speculation needs to be carefully monitored between the 19th and 25th if you're thinking is unclear, or you may have a bee in your bonnet and want to prove a point. This is not an intelligent way to spend your money and you're better to hold off and do some paper trading if the stock market seems appealing. But remember, this is still a glorified form of gambling and, unless you've researched your topic thoroughly, you should leave it to the experts and possibly get someone with knowledge in this area to manage your funds for you.

Between the 26th and 30th I detect opportunities to mix with some powerful people who can radically alter not only your way of thinking but your life objectives. Your fascination with power, money and prestige will be strong but try to keep things in perspective and realise that with power comes additional responsibility. Keeping up with the Jones's should never be the basis upon which you make important life decisions. Try to nurture and maintain a little 'contentment'; this is an often-ignored form of 'wealth'.

Romance and friendship

You mustn't get off to a poor start in your relationships by provoking others with your investigative style on the 2nd. Mercury no doubt makes you clever and correct but do you want to be right or improve your relationships? Don't hammer the point home, and give others the chance to speak as well.

VIRGO

You can be a little overpowering in your affections on the 11th or vice versa. Someone you love or admire may be smothering you with affection. On the 16th, you may start to question their motivation for doing so. Don't project your own attitude onto them and speak about how you feel, rather than putting up with it.

By the 14th you can stand out and really make your presence felt in some social circle. This is the return of the Sun to your birth position and revitalises you, giving you greater energy and a whole new sense of purpose. Use it well because you will attract even more new friends into your orb.

Your lover will support you after the 19th and there's a greater appreciation of who you are and this in turn will trigger you to support them, thereby reinforcing the relationship.

You'll become increasingly popular between the 17th and 20th and your communications are strong, particularly after the 23rd. During this cycle you can advertise yourself by dating online, and meeting others through the Internet and various electronic media will be a fascinating exercise.

You can be the voice of your friends after the 22nd when Mercury activates your powers of speech and persuasion. Anything you want you can ask for now and it's likely to be granted.

When Venus enters your Sun sign at this time, expect a lot of pleasure and affection but don't let apathy slip into the picture.

Work and money

Mercury is the ruler of your professional activities, and Uranus your zone of work. These planets are strong throughout the month of September and in particular finances should be satisfactory for you. You can come up with new ideas triggered by conversations you have with someone in the know. The danger here is that you may have just too many ideas, so picking the one that is best suited to you is the task at hand.

On the 6th and 7th you have an opportunity to re-evaluate the performance of your savings and possibly even rollover this money into another fund if you perceive you can get a better return on your money by way of higher interest.

Venus produces excellent social and financial opportunities for you around the 17th, perhaps with the chance for you to travel as part of your work duties to somewhere interstate.

On the 18th the Sun challenges your career and you may find yourself either stressed out or in a battle of wills with someone in a position of authority. Remember, it is a grave error to outshine the master.

The month finishes strongly with your public approval rating shooting up by the 30th.

Destiny dates

Positive: 3, 4, 5, 6, 7, 8, 14, 15, 16, 17, 26, 27, 28, 29, 30

Negative: 1

Mixed: 2, 11, 18, 19, 20, 22, 23

OCTOBER

Highlights of the month

You're under the magical influence of Venus and Mercury during the first part of October so my firm recommendation is to 'Make hay while the sun shines'.

Between the 1st and the 5th, your mind could be deeply engaged in thought, trying to work out solutions to problems that probably require more of an intuitive approach than a heavy duty intellectual exercise.

Your poetic abilities are strong this month and this is due to the combined influence of Venus and Mercury. Just speak your mind as honestly as you can and you'll be respected for it. You can mediate, persuade and sell something this month, whether an idea or an object.

The full Moon of the 4th brings you in touch with the deeper forces of nature and your emotional status could be a little volatile. Use this time wisely. Even the most intense states of mind have their own lessons for you.

Between the 10th and 13th you may hear some news that is upsetting. A friend or relative of a friend may undergo a serious or dangerous event. You may have to drop everything at a moment's notice to be there and help them through this troubling period. You may be chastised for doing so but trust your conscience because your loyalty is something you will not compromise.

You're going to need extra sleep this month. You could be worried or going through many different thought processes that will cause you to be restless, especially in the late hours of the night. Get a pen and pad handy so you can jot down your ideas and clear your mind.

New financial horizons present themselves after the 18th when the new Moon triggers some brilliant commercial flashes. If you've had a hobby that you've wanted to capitalise upon, why not consider doing it now?

Take extra precautions with cars and other machinery this month. You've only got yourself to blame if around the 20th you put your keys in the ignition and the engine won't start. The beauty of astrology is that when you are forewarned you are also forearmed. Be a step ahead of the event by booking your car in for a service if need be.

If your children are now in their late teens or early twenties, issues surrounding some of their decisions in life will need to be jointly managed by you. Education or new work projects will be a challenge for them, but your timely advice can help steer them in the right direction. Give them as much time as you can between the 23rd and 26th. This is also a great way to bond with them.

Romance and friendship

On the 1st and 2nd your energy levels will go through the roof. Everyone will notice this and your words will be just as powerful as your health.

You'll be highly strung around the 5th when Mercury and Uranus enter into challenge and this will affect your relationships in an unpredictable way. You and your partner will be out

VIRGO

of sync. Fortunately by the 8th your thinking will have slowed down and you'll be more able to regain some balance.

You can successfully schedule that deep and meaningful discussion with your lover because Venus will also make you charming enough to win over the hardest sceptic.

You can feel excited on the 10th and also the 11th when you want to break free of any limitations in your relationships. You're likely to do something completely out of character and run away into the arms of a new and exciting bunch of people.

The 13th is a cool day emotionally so don't expect too much fiery passion from your lover. This cycle is one in which you have to work extremely hard to get the attention that you desperately desire.

In contrast, on the 15th you'll be surprised when your partner lavishes heaps of attention on you. Lap it up, because this is what you've been after, isn't it?

The unwanted attention of someone between the 16th and 24th is a nuisance value. You could be stalked or harassed by an unwelcome admirer. Put your foot down and tell them how you feel.

Between the 26th and the 30th it is unwise for you to suppress how you feel. Don't bottle up your feelings because you're afraid of saying something. This will adversely affect your health, so speak up!

Work and money

Others could be forgiven for thinking you're a mad genius on the 4th. Your ideas will be bright, original but not necessarily accepted by them. You'll also have to apply your intuition to managing the workload.

You have to organise yourself better between the 9th and 11th. Get as much information as you can to start considering your long-term career objectives.

2009: OCTOBER

After the 15th your commercial activities will increase. You'll be quick in converting your ideas into profit and should see an increase in your income.

Around the 16th it's important to listen to the space between the words rather than what's being said. There'll be some hidden messages in what's being told to you, so get into the game and use it to your advantage.

After the 22nd you're likely to have the odd run-in with your employer if you're not careful. If you've been given the go-ahead to make decisions on behalf of the group, you could be thwarted and then wonder why you were given the all clear in the first place. You may need to spend time aside with your boss to clear up any misunderstandings.

Negotiations go well for you between the 23rd and 30th. Tie up loose ends with any contracts or paperwork.

Destiny dates

Positive: 3, 4, 8, 9, 15

Negative: 17, 19, 20, 21

Mixed: 1, 2, 5, 10, 11, 12, 13, 16, 18, 22, 23, 24, 25, 26, 27, 28, 29, 30

NOVEMBER

Highlights of the month

You can lead a horse to water but you can't necessarily make it drink. This sums up one of the key issues this month, particularly in reference to a friend whose problem can be clearly seen and solved but who may not necessarily take the advice you offer. After the 2nd you'll realise that your ethical or moral viewpoints will not be subscribed to by others. Quietly offer your advice and leave it at that.

On the 6th this issue may rear its head again when a third party, perhaps another friend, aligns themself with you on this matter. Remain discreet and my suggestion is not to share private information with third parties.

Dynamic Mars is moving through a low-key phase throughout November but just because your physical activities are lessened doesn't mean your mind will be any less active. You are more likely to be working behind the scenes, planning and strategising rather than rushing out madly before you've thought things through. This is good.

Between the 8th and the 15th, things will work well for you in all departments of your life. Saturn will also meander into your finance zone and you're likely to be much more practical about things. As a Virgo, practicality is your second name, but you'll be surprised at just how much more financially efficient you'll be.

Communications are high on your agenda and, with Mercury and the Sun doing the tango in your zone of communications, your to-do list will probably be as long as your arm. Be more efficient with your words because by the new Moon of the 16th you'll have figured out a fresh new system whereby you can make contact with quite a few people and save considerable time. There's a hint that your knowledge of the Internet, computers, e-mail and other communication devices will take a flying leap into the realm of expertise.

Home affairs, property and other transactions associated with your living space will start to emerge. Some effective planning should be done in this area as well because next month you'll want to act upon these bright sparks.

It often happens that relatives, particularly brothers and sisters or a spouse or loved ones, become a problem—on an ongoing basis as well. Between the 19th and 25th you can smooth over your difficult relations with them and lift your personal life to a new level. The lunar transit after the 27th shows the month finishes on an intimate level with some quiet times fulfilling you in some very unusual and sensual ways.

Romance and friendship

Once you've cleared the air from a romantic hassle, a period of readjustment is necessary and that's what's likely to happen, particularly between the 2nd and 6th. After the 10th you'll be feeling more confident and able to revive those cooling emotions.

On the 11th it might be easy to stretch the truth so as to not have to deal with some of the more uncomfortable aspects of your personal life. Try not to do this as it can send mixed messages to others.

VIRGO

You'll be more interested in talking about love between the 13th and the 15th. In fact, the new Moon of the 16th brings with it a whole new level of fantasy. You'll also find friends more co-operative and this harmonious balance of give and take, talking and listening, will really put you back into a more positive frame of mind.

When Mercury shifts gear and moves into your fourth zone of family life, you'll have a strong desire to get together with family members to reminisce about past events, both happy and sad. This is a perfect opportunity to resolve any longstanding differences.

There could be a few discussions around the 19th and 20th that centre on personal and possibly uncomfortable issues. It's worthwhile to release this energy, clear the air and move on.

Between the 19th and 25th, you'll be pushing your partner to explore the different frontiers of love and sexuality, but they may be a little too afraid to delve into their unconsciousness. You'll have to think of an angle to sell them the benefits of being a little bolder and more risqué.

Between the 29th and 30th your mind will be concerned more with dignity and honour and sticking to your ethical standards. By shutting down your brain to the consequences of your actions, you'll be doing yourself and your loved ones a disservice.

Work and money

It may be a little difficult to even get out of bed with Mars degrading your energy levels this month. You might have a little more luck after the 8th when the Moon connects with Mars, but even then much of your energy will be behind the scenes working at planning and problem solving.

On the 9th you're warned not to promise more than you can deliver as you may be completely unaware of the ramifications.

A workmate or business partner is unable to fulfil their part of the bargain after the 12th. You've only got yourself to blame if you haven't spoken up sooner about your dissatisfaction with these issues. A turn for the better can be expected on the 27th when Mercury and Mars cause you to see the light again, professionally speaking. Excellent omens indicate the opportunity to close a new deal with a brand new set of conditions.

Throw your hat in the ring on the 29th when the popularity stakes will be high and you have excellent friends who will rally around to your way of thinking. If there is some competitive situation in your workplace, you're more than likely to be successful in coming out number one.

Destiny dates

Positive: 8, 9, 10, 12, 13, 14, 15, 16, 21, 22, 23, 24, 25, 27

Negative: 29, 30

Mixed: 1, 2, 3, 4, 5, 6, 11, 19, 20

DECEMBER

Highlights of the month

This month you'll be gathering all your energies to cement your relationships on the domestic front. If you've neglected your family or been too absorbed in work, the period of the 1st to the 12th sees you making considerably more effort to turn things around.

Expressing yourself through home improvements, renovations and other cosmetic modifications on your home will not only improve things in your relationships but will add value to your property as well.

It's as if you're feeling much more satisfied in your relationships during this cycle and, even if you're not that way inclined, you might find yourself developing a taste for decorating, landscaping or even simply cooking in the kitchen. This might not be a long-lasting influence; but hey, what the heck? Enjoy it while it lasts.

Between the 8th and 13th you have a chance to revise some of your career objectives. Talk about your proposed changes with your loved ones before presenting your findings to your employers. It's best not to do things in secret as others may have a different idea to you and you don't want to be alarming anyone with radical changes out of the blue.

Try to avoid any form of manipulation, particularly with finances in this last month of the year. Be transparent and open about all of your objectives and intentions. The new Moon of the 16th up until the 25th will ensure open and harmonious communications, and relationships should be wonderfully satisfying for the festive season.

Some Virgos may opt to take on a second job during this time of great change. My only suggestion is that you're probably best to wait until the new year so you don't excessively stress yourself out by doing too much.

Don't let petty differences come between you and your mate around the 22nd. If you have personal goals, try to put them aside while you work through any differences. Sort out your romantic and marital difficulties before the completion of the year. This is a must.

The Moon ends its cycle on December 31st in your zone of life fulfillment and social friendships. This is an excellent reflection that what you'd hope to achieve in 2009 is likely to be realised to the max. It also completes its journey with powerful connections to one of your karmic planets. The fruits of your past actions yield great results and give you a new foundation from which to enter 2010.

Feel confident, Virgo. Be happy. The year 2009 is a wonderful one for you to celebrate your successes and new opportunities.

Romance and friendship

Expect many fun times during December, especially when Mercury moves into the romantic zone of your horoscope on the 6th. This is a playful period, bringing with it renewed vitality and desire. This cycle should continue quite strongly throughout the month and is supported by the Sun's entry into the same position on the 22nd, just before Christmas.

VIRGO

Excellent social and romantic vibrations occur on the 11th, 14th, 15th, 16th and the 17th, but you may choose to do something that affects your work adversely around the 18th when your sense of fun wins out over duty.

A new love affair can commence around the 17th, with Venus and Mars acting in concert to offer you another shot at it. This also smacks of a clandestine affair if you're already currently in a relationship, so do be careful of who and where you meet. It's probably better to keep your friendships out in the open.

Your social life is whacky between the 20th and 21st, with Venus and Uranus letting you know that it's A-okay to be completely mad, as long as it's done in a harmless way.

The Sun comes into contact with Pluto around the 25th, with Venus entering your zone of romance on the 26th. This is a great time to share your love with someone whom you consider worthy of the best you have to give. Perhaps during these last few days of the year, doing this would be the best gift that the universe could offer, would it not?

As the year rolls on to a close, the Moon completes its cycle in your zone of friendships. Your past karmic planet indicates a forgotten friend coming out of the woodwork at the eleventh hour, just when you least expect it.

Work and money

It's true that you'll have a lot of fun socially this month, but you mustn't overlook the need to complete your duties as promised because it would be easy to be distracted, especially between the 3rd and 5th.

The problem you have this month as far as work is concerned is that Mars continues to lie low in your zone of secrets and hidden activities. You won't want to be in the limelight and may even opt to finish your working year a little

2009: DECEMBER

earlier than normal. That's a good idea as I always recommend a holiday should be taken when the planetary cycles are reflecting a low energy level or lesser drive than usual.

You can complete any financial transactions or pay outstanding bills on the 9th, 10th, 19th and 20th, it's better to get that off your mind so you can enjoy the Christmas break much more freely.

Once you get through the final phase of professional difficulty on the 17th, it's smooth sailing for you. Tackling your employer over the last annoying issue is also not a bad idea so that your mind is completely free and prepared to enjoy fully the Christmas festivities.

Mercury goes retrograde on the 27th so the clear message at the end of the year is to shut down, unwind, and put aside your professional duties until the new year.

Destiny dates

Positive: 1, 2, 4, 6, 7, 8, 9, 10, 11, 12, 13, 14, 15, 16, 17, 18, 19, 20, 21, 25, 26, 31

Negative: Nil

Mixed: 3, 5, 22, 27

VIRGO

2009: Astronumerology

> *After all is said and done, a lot more will have been said than done.*
>
> —Anonymous

The power behind your name

By adding the numbers of your name you can see which planet is ruling you. Each of the letters of the alphabet is assigned a number, which is tabled below. These numbers are ruled by the planets. This is according to the ancient Chaldean system of numerology and is very different to the Pythagorean system to which many refer.

Each number is assigned a planet:

AIQJY	=	1	Sun
BKR	=	2	Moon
CGLS	=	3	Jupiter
DMT	=	4	Uranus
EHNX	=	5	Mercury
UVW	=	6	Venus
OZ	=	7	Neptune
FP	=	8	Saturn
—	=	9	Mars

Notice that the number 9 is not allotted a letter because it is considered special. Once the numbers have been added you will see that a single planet rules your name and personal affairs. Many famous actors, writers and musicians change their names to attract the energy of a luckier planet. You can experiment with the table and try new names or add letters of your second name to see how that vibration suits you. It's a lot of fun!

Here is an example of how to find out the power of your name. If your name is John Smith, calculate the ruling planet by correlating each letter to a number in the table like this:

J O H N S M I T H

1 7 5 5 3 4 1 4 5

Now add the numbers like this:

1 + 7 + 5 + 5 + 3 + 4 + 1 + 4 + 5 = 35

Then add 3 + 5 = 8

The ruling number of John Smith's name is 8, which is ruled by Saturn. Now study the name-number table to reveal the power of your name. The numbers 3 and 5 will also play a secondary role in John's character and destiny so in this case you would also study the effects of Jupiter and Mercury.

Name-number table

Your name number	Ruling planet	Your name characteristics
1	Sun	Charismatic personality. Great vitality and life force. Physically active and outgoing. Attracts good friends and individuals in powerful positions. Good government connections. Intelligent, dramatic, showy and successful. A loyal number for relationships.
2	Moon	Soft, emotional temperament. Changeable moods but psychic, intuitive senses. Imaginative nature and compassionate expression of feelings. Loves family, mother and home life. Night owl who probably needs more sleep.

VIRGO

		Success with the public and/or the opposite sex.
3	Jupiter	Outgoing, optimistic number with lucky overtones. Attracts opportunities without trying. Good sense of timing. Religious or spiritual aspirations. Can investigate the meaning of life. Loves to travel and explore the world and people.
4	Uranus	Explosive personality with many quirky aspects. Likes the untried and untested. Forward thinking, with many unusual friends. Gets bored easily so needs plenty of stimulating experiences. Innovative, technological and creative. Wilful and stubborn when wants to be. Unexpected events in life may be positive or negative.
5	Mercury	Quick-thinking mind with great powers of speech. Extremely active life; always on the go and lives on nervous energy. Youthful attitude and never grows old. Looks younger than actual age. Young friends and humorous disposition. Loves reading and writing.
6	Venus	Charming personality. Graceful and attractive character, who cherishes friends and social life. Musical or artistic interests. Good for money making as well as numerous love affairs. Career in

2009: ASTRONUMEROLOGY

		the public eye is possible. Loves family but is often overly concerned by friends.
7	Neptune	Intuitive, spiritual and self-sacrificing nature. Easily duped by those who need help. Loves to dream of life's possibilities. Has healing powers. Dreams are revealing and prophetic. Loves the water and will have many journeys in life. Spiritual aspirations dominate worldly desires.
8	Saturn	Hard-working, focused individual with slow but certain success. Incredible concentration and self-sacrifice for a goal. Money orientated but generous when trust is gained. Professional but may be a hard taskmaster. Demands highest standards and needs to learn to enjoy life a little more.
9	Mars	Incredible physical drive and ambition. Sports and outdoor activities are keys to health. Combative and likes to work and play just as hard. Protective of family, friends and territory. Individual tastes in life but is also self-absorbed. Needs to listen to others' advice to gain greater success.

VIRGO

Your 2009 planetary ruler

Astrology and numerology are closely linked. Each planet rules over a number between 1 and 9. Both your name and your birth date are ruled by planetary energies. Here are the planets and their ruling numbers:

1 Sun; 2 Moon; 3 Jupiter; 4 Uranus; 5 Mercury; 6 Venus; 7 Neptune; 8 Saturn; 9 Mars

Simply add the numbers of your birth date and the year in question to find out which planet will control the coming year for you. Here is an example:

If you were born on 12 November, add the numerals 1 and 2 (12, your day of birth) and 1 and 1 (11, your month of birth) to the year in question, in this case 2009 (current year), like this:

Add 1 + 2 + 1 + 1 + 2 + 0 + 0 + 9 = 16

Then add these numbers again: 1 + 6 = 7

The planet ruling your individual karma for 2009 will be Neptune because this planet rules the number 7.

You can even take your ruling name number as shown on page 111 and add it to the year in question to throw more light on your coming personal affairs like this:

John Smith = 8

Year coming = 2009

Add 8 + 2 + 0 + 0 + 9 = 19

Add 1 + 9 = 10

Add 1 + 0 = 1

This is the ruling year number using your name number as a basis. Therefore, study the Sun's (number 1) influence for 2009. Enjoy!

1 = Year of the Sun

Overview

The Sun is the brightest object in the heavens and rules number 1 and the sign of Leo. Because of this the coming year will bring you great success and popularity.

You'll be full of life and radiant vibrations and are more than ready to tackle your new nine-year cycle, which begins now. Any new projects you commence are likely to be successful.

Your health and vitality will be very strong and your stamina at its peak. Even if you happen to have the odd problem with your health, your recuperative power will be strong.

You have tremendous magnetism this year so social popularity won't be a problem for you. I see many new friends and lovers coming into your life. Expect loads of invitations to parties and fun-filled outings. Just don't take your health for granted as you're likely to burn the candle at both ends.

With success coming your way, don't let it go to your head. You must maintain humility, which will make you even more popular in the coming year.

Love and pleasure

This is an important cycle for renewing your love and connections with your family, particularly if you have children. The Sun is connected with the sign of Leo and therefore brings an increase in musical and theatrical activities. Entertainment and other creative hobbies will be high on your agenda and bring you a great sense of satisfaction.

Work

You won't have to make too much effort to be successful this year as the brightness of the Sun will draw opportunities to you. Changes in work are likely and if you have been concerned that opportunities are few and far between, 2009 will be different. You can expect some sort of promotion or an increase in income because your employers will take special note of your skills and service orientation.

Improving your luck

Leo is the ruler of number 1 and therefore, if you're born under this star sign, 2009 will be particularly lucky. For others, July and August, the months of Leo, will bring good fortune. The 1st, 8th, 15th and 22nd hours of Sundays especially will give you a unique sort of luck in any sort of competition or activities generally. Keep your eye out for those born under Leo as they may be able to contribute something to your life and may even have a karmic connection to you. This is a particularly important year for your destiny.

Your lucky numbers in this coming cycle are 1, 10, 19 and 28.

2 = Year of the Moon

Overview

There's nothing more soothing than the cool light of the full Moon on a clear night. The Moon is emotional and receptive and controls your destiny in 2009. If you're able to use the positive energies of the Moon, it will be a great year in which you can realign and improve your relationships, particularly with family members.

Making a commitment to becoming a better person and bringing your emotions under control will also dominate your thinking. Try not to let your emotions get the better of you throughout the coming year because you may be drawn into the changeable nature of these lunar vibrations as well. If you fail to keep control of your emotional life you'll later regret some of your actions. You must carefully blend thinking with feeling to arrive at the best results. Your luck throughout 2009 will certainly be determined by the state of your mind.

2009: ASTRONUMEROLOGY

Because the Moon and the sign of Cancer rule the number 2 there is a certain amount of change to be expected this year. Keep your feelings steady and don't let your heart rule your head.

Love and pleasure

Your primary concern in 2009 will be your home and family life. You'll be keen to finally take on those renovations, or work on your garden. You may even think of buying a new home. You can at last carry out some of those plans and make your dreams come true. If you find yourself a little more temperamental than usual, do some extra meditation and spend time alone until you sort this out. You mustn't withhold your feelings from your partner as this will only create frustration.

Work

During 2009 your focus will be primarily on feelings and family; however, this doesn't mean you can't make great strides in your work as well. The Moon rules the general public and what you might find is that special opportunities and connections with the world at large present themselves to you. You could be working with large numbers of people.

If you're looking for a better work opportunity, try to focus your attention on women who can give you a hand. Use your intuition as it will be finely tuned this year. Work and career success depends upon your instincts.

Improving your luck

The sign of Cancer is your ruler this year and because the Moon rules Mondays, both this day of the week and the month of July are extremely lucky for you. The 1st, 8th, 15th and 22nd hours on Mondays will be very powerful. Pay special attention to the new and full Moon days throughout 2009.

The numbers 2, 11 and 29 are lucky for you.

3 = Year of Jupiter

Overview

The year 2009 will be a 3 year for you and, because of this, Jupiter and Sagittarius will dominate your affairs. This is very lucky and shows that you'll be motivated to broaden your horizons, gain more money and become extremely popular in your social circles. It looks like 2009 will be a fun-filled year with much excitement.

Jupiter and Sagittarius are generous to a fault and so likewise, your open-handedness will mark the year. You'll be friendly and helpful to all of those around you.

Pisces is also under the rulership of the number 3 and this brings out your spiritual and compassionate nature. You'll become a much better person, reducing your negative karma by increasing your self-awareness and spiritual feelings. You will want to share your luck with those you love.

Love and pleasure

Travel and seeking new adventures will be part and parcel of your romantic life this year. Travelling to distant lands and meeting unusual people will open your heart to fresh possibilities of romance.

You'll try novel and audacious things and will find yourself in a different circle of friends. Compromise will be important in making your existing relationships work. Talk about your feelings. If you are currently in a relationship you'll feel an upswing in your affection for your partner. This is a perfect opportunity to deepen your love for each other and take your relationship to a new level.

If you're not attached to someone just yet, there's good news for you. Great opportunities lie in store for you and a spiritual or karmic connection may be experienced in 2009.

Work

Great fortune can be expected through your working life in the next twelve months. Your friends and work colleagues will want to help you achieve your goals. Even your employers will be amenable to your requests for extra money or a better position within the organisation.

If you want to start a new job or possibly begin an independent line of business this is a great year to do it. Jupiter looks set to give you plenty of opportunities, success and a superior reputation.

Improving your luck

As long as you can keep a balanced view of things and not overdo anything, your luck will increase dramatically throughout 2009. The important thing is to remain grounded and not be too airy-fairy about your objectives. Be realistic about your talents and capabilities and don't brag about your skills or achievements. This will only invite envy from others.

Moderate your social life as well and don't drink or eat too much as this will slow your reflexes and lessen your chances for success.

You have plenty of spiritual insights this year so you should use them to their maximum. In the 1st, 8th, 15th and 24th hours of Thursdays you should use your intuition to enhance your luck, and the numbers 3, 12, 21 and 30 are also lucky for you. March and December are your lucky months but generally the whole year should go pretty smoothly for you.

4 = Year of Uranus

Overview

The electric and exciting planet of the zodiac Uranus and its sign of Aquarius rule your affairs throughout 2009. Dramatic

VIRGO

events will surprise and at the same time unnerve you in your professional and personal life. So be prepared!

You'll be able to achieve many things this year and your dreams are likely to come true, but you mustn't be distracted or scattered with your energies. You'll be breaking through your own self-limitations and this will present challenges from your family and friends. You'll want to be independent and develop your spiritual powers and nothing will stop you.

Try to maintain discipline and an orderly lifestyle so you can make the most of these special energies this year. If unexpected things do happen, it's not a bad idea to have an alternative plan so you don't lose momentum.

Love and pleasure

You want something radical, something different in your relationships this year. It's quite likely that your love life will be feeling a little less than exciting so you'll take some important steps to change that. If your partner is as progressive as you'll be this year, then your relationship is likely to improve and fulfil both of you.

In your social life you will meet some very unusual people whom you'll feel are specially connected to you spiritually. You may want to ditch everything for the excitement and passion of a completely new relationship, but tread carefully as this may not work out exactly as you'd expected.

Work

Technology, computing and the Internet will play a larger role in your professional life this coming year. You'll have to move ahead with the times and learn new skills if you want to achieve success.

A hectic schedule is likely, so make sure your diary is with you at all times. Try to be more efficient and don't waste time.

New friends and alliances at work will help you achieve even greater success in the coming period. Becoming a team player will be even more important towards gaining satisfaction in your professional endeavours.

Improving your luck

Moving too quickly and impulsively will cause you problems on all fronts, so be a little more patient and think your decisions through more carefully. Social, romantic and professional opportunities will come to you but take a little time to investigate the ramifications of your actions.

The 1st, 8th, 15th and 20th hours of any Saturday are lucky, but love and luck are likely to cross your path when you least expect it. The numbers 4, 13, 22 and 31 are also lucky for you this year.

5 = Year of Mercury

Overview

The supreme planet of communication, Mercury, is your ruling planet throughout 2009. The number 5, which is connected to Mercury, will confer upon you success through your intellectual abilities.

Any form of writing or speaking will be improved and this will be, to a large extent, underpinning your success. Your imagination will be stimulated by this planet with many incredible new and exciting ideas coming to mind.

Mercury and the number 5 are considered somewhat indecisive. Be firm in your attitude and don't let too many ideas or opportunities distract and confuse you. By all means get as much information as you can to help you make the right decision.

I see you involved with money proposals, job applications, even contracts that need to be signed so remain clear-headed as much as possible.

VIRGO

Your business skills and clear and concise communication will be at the heart of your life in 2009.

Love and pleasure

Mercury, which rules the signs of Gemini and Virgo, will make your love life a little difficult due to its changeable nature. On the one hand you'll feel passionate and loving to your partner, yet on the other you will feel like giving it all up for the excitement of a new affair. Maintain the middle ground.

Also, try not to be too critical with your friends and family members. The influence of Virgo makes you prone to expecting much more from others than they're capable of giving. Control your sharp tongue and don't hurt people's feelings. Encouraging others is the better path, leading to more emotional satisfaction.

Work

Speed will dominate your professional life in 2009. You'll be flitting from one subject to another and taking on far more than you can handle. You'll need to make some serious changes in your routine to handle the avalanche of work that will come your way. You'll also be travelling with your work, but not necessarily overseas.

If you're in a job you enjoy then this year will give you additional successes. If not, it may be time to move on.

Improving your luck

Communication is the secret of attaining your desires in the coming twelve months. Keep focused on one idea rather than scattering your energies in all directions and your success will be speedier.

By looking after your health, sleeping well and exercising regularly, you'll build up your resilience and mental strength.

The 1st, 8th, 15th and 20th hours of Wednesday are lucky so it's best to schedule your meetings and other important social engagements during these times. The lucky numbers for Mercury are 5, 14, 23 and 32.

6 = Year of Venus

Overview

Because you're ruled by 6 this year, love is in the air! Venus, Taurus and Libra are well known for their affinity with romance, love, and even marriage. If ever you were going to meet a soulmate and feel comfortable in love, 2009 must surely be your year.

Taurus has a strong connection to money and practical affairs as well, so finances will also improve if you are diligent about work and security issues.

The important thing to keep in mind this year is that sharing love and making that important soul connection should be kept high on your agenda. This will be an enjoyable period in your life.

Love and pleasure

Romance is the key thing for you this year and your current relationships will become more fulfilling if you happen to be attached. For singles, a 6 year heralds an important meeting that eventually leads to marriage.

You'll also be interested in fashion, gifts, jewellery and all sorts of socialising. It's at one of these social engagements that you could meet the love of your life. Remain available!

Venus is one of the planets that has a tendency to overdo things, so be moderate in your eating and drinking. Try generally to maintain a modest lifestyle.

VIRGO

Work

You'll have a clearer insight into finances and your future security during a number 6 year. Whereas you may have had additional expenses and extra distractions previously, your mind will be more settled and capable of longer-term planning along these lines.

With the extra cash you might see this year, decorating your home or office will give you a special sort of satisfaction.

Social affairs and professional activities will be strongly linked. Any sort of work-related functions may offer you romantic opportunities as well. On the other hand, be careful not to mix up your workplace relationships with romantic ideals. This could complicate some of your professional activities.

Improving your luck

You'll want more money and a life of leisure and ease in 2009. Keep working on your strengths and eliminate your negative personality traits to create greater luck and harmony in your life.

Moderate all your actions and don't focus exclusively on money and material objects. Feed your spiritual needs as well. By balancing the inner and outer you'll see that your romantic and professional life will be enhanced more easily.

The 1st, 8th, 15th and 20th hours on Fridays will be very lucky for you and new opportunities will arise for you at those times. You can use the numbers 6, 15, 24 and 33 to increase luck in your general affairs.

7 = Year of Neptune

Overview

The last and most evolved sign of the zodiac is Pisces, which is ruled by Neptune. The number 7 is deeply connected with this zodiacal sign and governs you in 2009. Your ideals seem to be clearer and more spiritually orientated than ever before. Your desire to evolve and understand your inner self will be a double-edged sword. It depends on how organised you are as to how well you can use these spiritual and abstract concepts in your practical life.

Your past emotional hurts and deep emotional issues will be dealt with and removed for good, if you are serious about becoming a better human being.

Spend a little more time caring for yourself rather than others, as it's likely some of your friends will drain you of energy with their own personal problems. Of course, you mustn't turn a blind eye to the needs of others, but don't ignore your own personal needs in the process.

Love and pleasure

Meeting people with similar life views and spiritual aspirations will rekindle your faith in relationships. If you do choose to develop a new romance, make sure that there is a clear understanding of the responsibilities of one to the other. Don't get swept off your feet by people who have ulterior motives.

Keep your relationships realistic and see that the most idealistic partnerships must eventually come down to Earth. Deal with the practicalities of life.

Work

This is a year of hard work, but one in which you'll come to understand the deeper significance of your professional ideals. You may discover a whole new aspect to your career, which involves a more compassionate and self-sacrificing side to your personality.

You'll also find that your way of working will change and that you'll be more focused and able to get into the spirit of whatever you do. Finding meaningful work is very likely and therefore this could be a year when money, security, creativity and spirituality overlap to bring you a great sense of personal satisfaction.

Tapping into your greater self through meditation and self-study will bring you great benefits throughout 2009.

Improving your luck

Using self-sacrifice along with discrimination will be an unusual method of improving your luck. The laws of karma state that what you give, you receive in greater measure. This is one of the principal themes for you in 2009.

The 1st, 8th, 15th and 20th hours of Tuesdays are your lucky times. The numbers 7, 16, 25 and 34 should be used to increase your lucky energies.

8 = Year of Saturn

Overview

The earthy and practical sign of Capricorn and its ruler Saturn are intimately linked to the number 8, which rules you in 2009. Your discipline and far-sightedness will help you achieve great things in the coming year. With cautious discernment, slowly but surely you will reach your goals.

It may be that due to the influence of the solitary Saturn, your best work and achievement will be behind closed doors away from the limelight. You mustn't fear this as you'll discover many new things about yourself. You'll learn just how strong you really are.

Love and pleasure

Work will overshadow your personal affairs in 2009, but you mustn't let this erode the personal relationships you have. Becoming a workaholic brings great material successes but will

2009: ASTRONUMEROLOGY

also cause you to become too insular and aloof. Your family members won't take too kindly to you working 100-hour weeks.

Responsibility is one of the key words for this number and you will therefore find yourself in a position of authority that leaves very little time for fun. Try to make time to enjoy the company of friends and family and by all means schedule time off on the weekends as it will give you the peace of mind you're looking for.

Because of your responsible attitude it will be very hard for you not to assume a greater role in your workplace and this indicates longer working hours with the likelihood of a promotion with equally good remuneration.

Work

Money is high on your agenda in 2009. Number 8 is a good money number according to the Chinese and this year is at last likely to bring you the fruits of your hard labour. You are cautious and resourceful in all your dealings and will not waste your hard-earned savings. You will also be very conscious of using your time wisely.

You will be given more responsibilities and you're likely to take them on, if only to prove to yourself that you can handle whatever life dishes up.

Expect a promotion in which you will play a leading role in your work. Your diligence and hard work will pay off, literally, in a bigger salary and more respect from others.

Improving your luck

Caution is one of the key characteristics of the number 8 and is linked to Capricorn. But being overly cautious could cause you to miss valuable opportunities. If an offer is put to you, try to think outside the square and balance it with your naturally cautious nature.

VIRGO

Be gentle and kind to yourself. By loving yourself, others will naturally love you, too. The 1st, 8th, 15th and 20th hours of Saturdays are exceptionally lucky for you as are the numbers 1, 8, 17, 26 and 35.

9 = Year of Mars

Overview

You are now entering the final year of a nine-year cycle dominated by the planet Mars and the sign of Aries. You'll be completing many things and are determined to be successful after several years of intense work.

Some of your relationships may now have reached their use-by date and even these personal affairs may need to be released. Don't let arguments and disagreements get in the road of friendly resolution in these areas of your life.

Mars is a challenging planet and, this year, although you will be very active and productive, you may find others trying to obstruct the achievement of your goals. As a result you may react strongly to them, thereby creating disharmony in your workplace. Don't be so impulsive or reckless, and generally slow things down. The slower, steadier approach has greater merit this year.

Love and pleasure

If you become too bossy and pushy with friends this year you will just end up pushing them out of your life. It's a year to end certain friendships but by the same token it could be the perfect time to end conflicts and thereby bolster your love affairs in 2009.

If you're feeling a little irritable and angry with those you love, try getting rid of these negative feelings through some intense, rigorous sports and physical activity. This will definitely relieve tension and improve your personal life.

2009: ASTRONUMEROLOGY

Work

Because you're healthy and able to work at a more intense pace you'll achieve an incredible amount in the coming year. Overwork could become a problem if you're not careful.

Because the number 9 and Mars are infused with leadership energy, you'll be asked to take the reins of the job and steer your company or group in a certain direction. This will bring with it added responsibility but also a greater sense of purpose for you.

Improving your luck

Because of the hot and restless energy of the number 9, it is important to create more mental peace in your life this year. Lower the temperature, so to speak, and decompress your relationships rather than becoming aggravated. Try to talk to your work partners and loved ones rather than telling them what to do. This will generally pick up your health and your relationships.

The 1st, 8th, 15th and 20th hours of Tuesdays are the luckiest for you this year and, if you're involved in any disputes or need to attend to health issues, these times are also very good for the best results. Your lucky numbers are 9, 18, 27 and 36.

VIRGO

2009:
Your Daily Planner

> *A failure is a man who has blundered, but is not able to cash in on the experience.*
>
> —Elbert Hubbard

There is a little-known branch of astrology called electional astrology, and it can help you select the most appropriate times for many of your day-to-day activities.

Ancient astrologers understood the planetary patterns and how they impacted on each of us. This allowed them to suggest the best possible times to start various important activities. Many farmers today still use this approach: they understand the phases of the Moon, and attest to the fact that planting seeds on certain lunar days produces a far better crop than planting on other days.

The following section covers many areas of daily life, and uses the cycles of the Moon and the combined strength of the other planets to work out the best times to start different types of activity.

So to create your own personal almanac, first select the activity you are interested in, and then quickly scan the year for the best months to start it. When you have selected the month, you can finetune your timing by finding the best specific dates. You can then be sure that the planetary energies will be in sync with you, offering you the best possible outcome.

Coupled with what you know about your monthly and weekly trends, the daily planner can be a powerful tool to help you capitalise on opportunities that come your way this year.

Good luck, and may the planets bless you with great success, fortune and happiness in 2009!

Starting activities

How many times have you made a new year's resolution to begin a diet or be a better person in your relationships? And

2009: YOUR DAILY PLANNER

how many times has it not worked out? Well, the reason may be partly that you started out at the wrong time! How successful you are is strongly influenced by the position of the Moon and the planets when you begin a particular activity. You could be more successful with the following activities if you start them on the days indicated.

Relationships

We all feel more empowered on some days than on others. This is because the planets have some power over us—their movement and their relationships to each other determine the ebb and flow of our energies. And our level of self-confidence and our sense of romantic magnetism play an important part in the way we behave in relationships.

Your daily planner tells you the ideal dates for meeting new friends, initiating a love affair, spending time with family and loved ones—it even tells you the most appropriate times for sexual encounters.

You'll be surprised at how much more impact you make in your relationships when you tune yourself in to the planetary energies on these special dates.

Falling in love/restoring love

During these times you could expect favourable energies to meet your soulmate or, if you've had difficulty in a relationship, to approach the one you love to rekindle both your and their emotional responses:

January	28, 30
February	25, 26
March	6, 7, 8, 28, 29, 30
April	25, 26, 30
May	1, 2, 5, 7, 26, 27, 28, 29

VIRGO

June	2, 3, 23, 24, 26, 29, 30
July	22, 23, 26, 27
August	14, 15, 16, 17, 22, 23, 24
September	10, 14, 16, 19, 20, 21
October	9, 10, 11, 12, 13
November	25, 26
December	22, 23, 27, 31

Special times with friends and family

Socialising, partying and having a good time with those you enjoy being with is highly favourable under the following dates. These dates are excellent to spend time with family and loved ones in a domestic environment:

January	26
February	8, 12, 13, 14, 22, 23, 24
March	8, 22, 23
April	19, 27, 28
May	1, 2, 15, 16, 17, 24, 25, 28, 29
June	2, 3, 11, 12, 13, 22, 30
July	23, 26, 27
August	5, 6, 23, 24
September	16
October	13
November	8, 10, 24
December	19, 20, 21, 29

Healing or resuming relationships

If you're trying to get back together with the one you love and need a heart-to-heart or deep and meaningful, you can try the following dates to do so:

January	5, 8, 11, 12, 18, 19, 20, 21, 22, 23, 24, 25, 26, 28, 30
February	8, 12, 13, 14
March	8
April	18, 19
May	1, 2, 28, 29
June	2, 3, 30
July	23, 26, 27
August	23, 24
September	16
October	13
November	8
December	22, 23, 27

Sexual encounters

Physical and sexual energies are well favoured on the following dates. The energies of the planets enhance your moments of intimacy during these times:

January	5, 30
February	25, 26
March	6, 7, 8, 28, 29, 30
April	25, 26, 30
May	1, 2, 5, 7, 26, 27, 28, 29

VIRGO

June	2, 3, 23, 24, 26, 29, 30
July	22, 23, 26, 27
August	23, 24
September	16
October	13
November	25, 26
December	22, 23, 27, 31

Health and wellbeing

Your aura and life force are susceptible to the movements of the planets; in particular, they respond to the phases of the Moon.

The following dates are the most appropriate times to begin a diet, have cosmetic surgery, or seek medical advice. They also tell you when the best times are to help others.

Feeling of wellbeing

Your physical as well as your mental alertness should be strong on these following dates. You can plan your activities and expect a good response from others:

January	8, 9, 26, 27
February	4, 5, 22, 23
March	31
April	18, 19, 27, 28
May	16, 17
June	21, 22
July	19
August	5, 6, 24, 25

September	12, 28, 30
October	8, 9
November	8, 10
December	19, 20, 21, 29, 30

Healing and medicine

This is good for approaching others who have expertise at a time when you need some deeper understanding. This is also favourable for any sort of healing or medication and making appointments with doctors or psychologists. Planning surgery around these dates should bring good results.

Often giving up our time and energy to assist others doesn't necessarily result in the expected outcome. By lending a helping hand to a friend on the following dates, the results should be favourable:

January	1, 20, 21, 22, 23, 24, 25, 26, 27, 28, 29, 30, 31
February	9, 10, 11, 12, 13, 14, 15, 16, 17, 18, 19, 20, 21, 22, 23, 24, 25, 26, 27, 28
March	2, 3, 4, 5, 6, 7, 8, 9, 22, 26, 28, 29, 30, 31
April	1, 10, 12, 15, 18, 20, 27, 28, 29, 30
May	1, 3, 7, 8, 9, 10, 11, 12
June	6, 7, 9, 13, 14, 15, 19, 21, 22
July	5, 6, 7, 8, 10, 12, 18, 19, 20, 25, 26
August	6, 7, 8, 9, 10, 29, 30, 31
September	1, 6, 27
October	8, 9, 10, 11, 12, 25, 26
November	18, 19, 20, 21, 22
December	10, 11, 12

VIRGO

Money

Money is an important part of life, and involves many decisions; decisions about borrowing, investing, spending. The ideal times for transactions are very much influenced by the planets, and whether your investment or nest egg grows or doesn't grow can often be linked to timing. Making your decisions on the following dates could give you a whole new perspective on your financial future.

Managing wealth and money

To build your nest egg, it's a good time to open your bank account and invest money on the following dates:

January	3, 4, 5, 10, 11, 16, 17, 23, 24, 25, 31
February	1, 6, 7, 12, 13, 14, 20, 21, 27, 28
March	5, 6, 7, 12, 13, 19, 26, 27
April	2, 3, 8, 9, 15, 17, 23, 24, 29, 30
May	5, 6, 7, 13, 14, 20, 21, 26, 27
June	2, 3, 9, 10, 16, 17, 18, 23, 24, 29, 30
July	6, 7, 8, 14, 15, 20, 21, 26, 27
August	2, 3, 4, 10, 11, 17, 18, 23, 24, 30, 31
September	6, 7, 13, 14, 19, 20, 26, 27
October	3, 4, 5, 10, 11, 16, 17, 18, 23, 24, 25, 31
November	1, 6, 7, 13, 14, 20, 21, 27, 28
December	4, 5, 10, 11, 17, 18, 24, 25, 26, 31

Spending

It's always fun to spend but the following dates are more in tune with this activity and are likely to give you better results:

2009: YOUR DAILY PLANNER

January	20, 28, 30
February	3
March	28, 29, 30
April	25, 26
May	31
June	1, 2, 7, 8, 9, 10, 28, 30
July	1, 2, 3, 26, 27, 29, 30
August	2, 3, 4, 5, 20, 21, 22, 23, 24, 25
September	19, 20, 21, 22, 23
October	9, 10
November	1, 7, 8, 17
December	27, 28

Selling

If you're thinking of selling something, whether it is small or large, consider the following dates as ideal times to do so:

January	3, 18, 19, 20, 21, 25, 26, 27, 28, 29, 30, 31
February	8, 10, 11, 12, 13, 14, 15, 18, 20, 22, 23, 24, 26, 28
March	2, 3, 4, 5, 6, 7, 8, 9, 16, 26, 27, 28, 31
April	5, 10, 19, 20, 23, 25, 27, 28, 29
May	1, 2, 7, 9, 13, 14, 21, 24, 25, 28, 29, 31
June	1, 2, 7, 8, 14, 16, 17, 20, 21, 22, 26, 30
July	1, 2, 3, 9, 10, 11, 15, 16, 17, 26, 27
August	2, 3, 4, 13, 14, 15, 16, 17
September	1, 2, 3, 4, 5, 6, 14, 15, 16, 17, 21, 22, 23, 24, 25, 26, 27, 28, 30, 31

VIRGO

October	1, 2, 3, 4, 5, 6, 7, 8, 9, 10, 11, 12, 31
November	2, 3, 9, 10, 11, 12, 13, 25, 26, 27, 28, 29, 30
December	1, 2, 3, 7, 8, 9, 17, 20

Borrowing

Few of us like to borrow money, but if you must, taking out a loan on the following dates should be positive:

January	11, 18, 19, 20, 23, 24, 25
February	15, 16, 20, 21
March	14, 15, 19, 20
April	10, 11, 12, 15, 16, 17
May	9, 13, 14
June	9, 10
July	7, 8, 20, 21
August	17, 18
September	13, 14
October	10, 11
November	6, 7, 15, 16
December	4, 5, 12, 13, 14

Work and education

Your career is important to you, and continual improvement of your skills is therefore also crucial, professionally, mentally and socially. The dates below will help you find out the most appropriate times to improve your professional talents and commence new work or education associated with your work.

You may need to decide when to start learning a new skill, when to ask for a promotion, and even when to make an

2009: YOUR DAILY PLANNER

important career change. Here are the days when mental and educational power is strong.

Learning new skills

Educational pursuits are lucky and bring good results on the following dates:

January	8, 9
February	4, 5
March	3, 4, 10, 31
April	1, 6, 7, 27, 28
May	3, 4, 25, 30, 31
June	1, 6, 7, 27, 28
July	4, 5, 24, 25, 31
August	1, 21, 22, 27, 28, 29
September	23, 24, 25
October	21, 22
November	17, 18, 19
December	29, 30

Changing career path or profession

If you're feeling stuck and need to move into a new professional activity, changing jobs can be done at these times:

January	6, 7
February	2, 3
March	1, 2, 3, 4, 5, 6, 7, 8, 9, 10, 28, 29, 30
April	6, 7, 25, 26
May	3, 4, 30, 31
June	1, 27, 28

VIRGO

July	6, 24, 25
August	2, 3, 4, 21, 22, 30, 31
September	26, 27
October	23, 24, 25
November	2, 20, 21, 29, 30
December	1, 17, 18, 27, 28

Promotion, professional focus and hard work

To increase your mental focus and achieve good results from the work you do, promotions are likely on these dates that follow:

January	4, 5, 6, 11, 12, 13, 14, 15, 16, 21
February	6
March	18, 19, 20
April	8, 28, 29
May	12, 21
June	25, 26
July	1, 2, 3, 8, 15, 17
August	4, 14, 15, 16, 17, 18, 22, 23, 24
September	14, 15, 18, 19, 23, 24, 25, 26
October	22
November	7, 10, 11, 12, 17
December	1, 2, 3, 7, 28

Travel

Setting out on a holiday or adventurous journey is exciting. To gain the most out of your holidays and journeys, travelling on the following dates is likely to give you a sense of fulfilment:

2009: YOUR DAILY PLANNER

January	9, 10, 28, 29, 30, 31
February	1, 4, 5, 26
March	3, 4, 5, 6, 7, 27, 31
April	27, 28, 29
May	1, 2, 25
June	6, 7, 25, 26
July	6, 31
August	1, 2, 21, 22, 23, 24, 29
September	19, 20, 23, 24, 25, 26, 27
October	1, 2, 3, 25, 28, 29, 30, 31
November	1, 17, 18, 26, 28
December	17, 18, 23, 26

Beauty and grooming

Believe it or not, cutting your hair or nails has a powerful effect on your body's electromagnetic energy. If you cut your hair or nails at the wrong time of the month, you can reduce your level of vitality significantly. Use these dates to ensure you optimise your energy levels by staying in tune with the stars.

Hair and nails

January	1, 2, 8, 9, 21, 22, 28, 29, 30
February	4, 5, 17, 18, 19, 25, 26
March	3, 4, 16, 17, 18, 24, 25, 31
April	1, 13, 14, 20, 21, 22, 27, 28, 29, 30
May	8, 10, 11, 12, 18, 19, 24, 25
June	6, 7, 8, 14, 15, 21, 22

VIRGO

July	4, 5, 11, 12, 13, 18, 19, 31
August	1, 7, 8, 9, 14, 15, 16, 27, 28, 29
September	4, 5, 11, 12, 23, 24, 25
October	1, 2, 8, 9, 21, 22, 28, 29, 30
November	4, 5, 17, 18, 19, 25, 26
December	2, 3, 15, 16, 22, 23, 29, 30

Therapies, massage and self-pampering

January	18, 19, 20, 26, 27
February	3, 6, 7, 8, 12, 13, 14, 15, 16, 22, 23, 24
March	6, 8, 28, 29, 30
April	5, 8, 9, 18, 19, 25, 26, 29, 30
May	1, 2, 5, 7, 9, 15, 16, 17, 22, 23, 26, 27, 28, 29
June	2, 3, 4, 5, 11, 12, 13, 19, 20, 23, 24, 26, 30
July	1, 2, 3, 9, 10, 23, 26, 27, 28, 29, 30
August	6, 12, 13, 17, 18, 19, 20, 23, 24, 25, 26
September	1, 2, 13, 14, 16
October	10, 11, 12, 13, 16, 17, 27
November	8, 9, 10, 13, 16, 23, 24, 29, 30
December	1, 4, 5, 6, 7, 10, 11, 12, 13, 14, 19, 20, 21, 27, 28, 31

MILLS & BOON
MODERN™

...International affairs, seduction and passion guaranteed

The Greek Tycoon's Pregnant Wife
Anne Mather

Miranda Lee
Blackmailed into the Italian's Bed

8 brand-new titles each month

Available on the first Friday of every month
from WHSmith, ASDA, Tesco
and all good bookshops
www.millsandboon.co.uk

GEN/01/RTL11

MILLS & BOON
MODERN
Heat

If you like Mills & Boon Modern you'll love Modern Heat!

Strong, sexy alpha heroes, sizzling storylines and exotic locations from around the world – what more could you want!

2 brand-new titles each month

Available on the first Friday of every month
from WHSmith, ASDA, Tesco
and all good bookshops
www.millsandboon.co.uk

MILLS & BOON
Romance

Pure romance, pure emotion

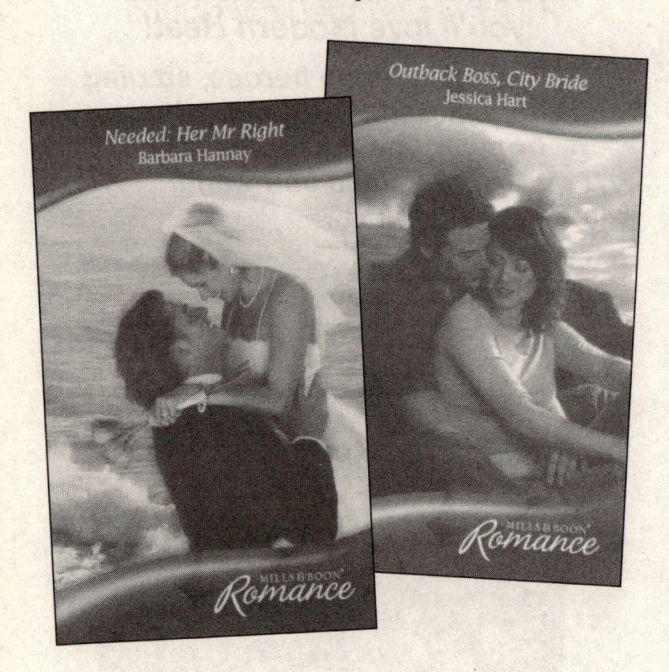

Needed: Her Mr Right
Barbara Hannay

Outback Boss, City Bride
Jessica Hart

4 brand-new titles each month

Available on the first Friday of every month
from WHSmith, ASDA, Tesco
and all good bookshops
www.millsandboon.co.uk

GEN/02/RTL11

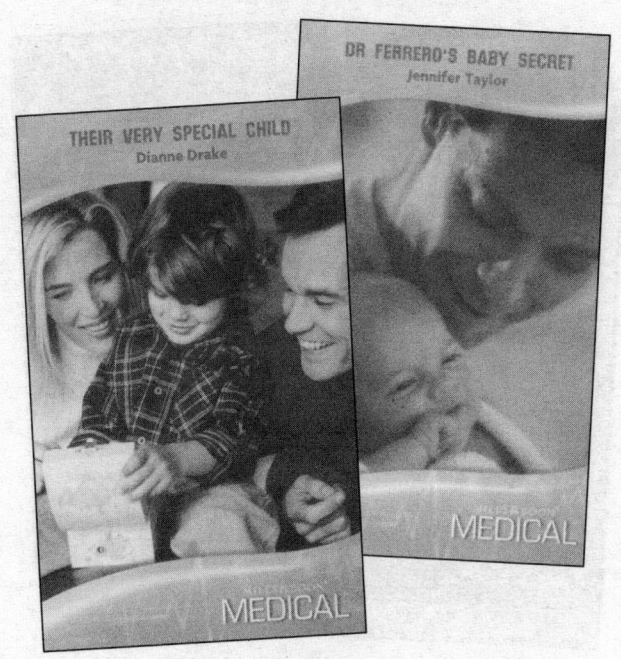

MILLS & BOON
Historical

Rich, vivid and passionate

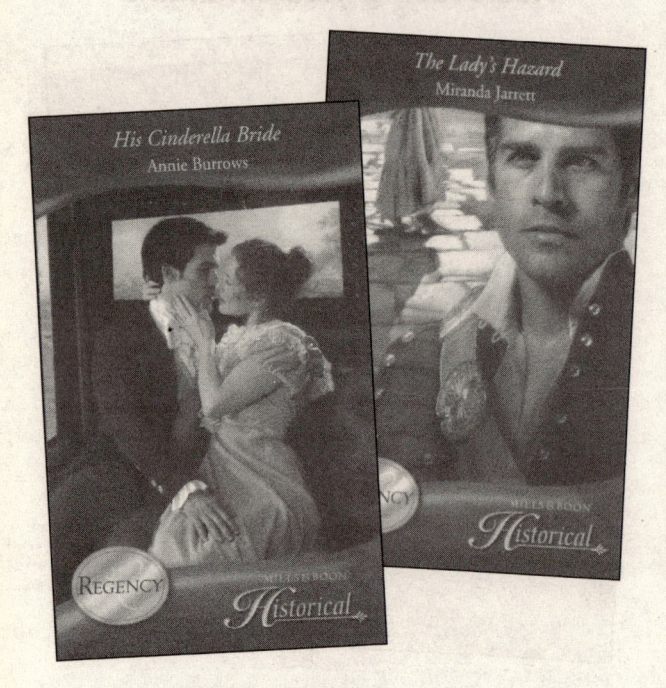

His Cinderella Bride
Annie Burrows

The Lady's Hazard
Miranda Jarrett

4 brand-new titles each month

Available on the first Friday of every month
from WHSmith, ASDA, Tesco
and all good bookshops
www.millsandboon.co.uk

GEN/04/RTL11

MILLS & BOON
Blaze

Scorching hot sexy reads...

4 brand-new titles each month

Available on the first Friday of every month
from WHSmith, ASDA, Tesco
and all good bookshops
www.millsandboon.co.uk

GEN/14/RTL11

MILLS & BOON
Special Edition

Life, love and family

6 brand-new titles each month

Available on the third Friday of every month
from WHSmith, ASDA, Tesco
and all good bookshops
www.millsandboon.co.uk

GEN/23/RTL11

MILLS & BOON
Super ROMANCE

Enjoy the drama, explore the emotions, experience the relationships

4 brand-new titles each month

Available on the third Friday of every month
from WHSmith, ASDA, Tesco
and all good bookshops
www.millsandboon.co.uk

GEN/38/RTL11

MILLS & BOON
INTRIGUE

Breathtaking romance & adventure

Survival Instinct
Doranna Durgin

Secret Weapon Spouse
BJ Daniels

8 brand-new titles each month

Available on the third Friday of every month
from WHSmith, ASDA, Tesco
and all good bookshops
www.millsandboon.co.uk

GEN/46/RTL11

MILLS & BOON
Desire™ 2-in-1

2 passionate, dramatic love stories in each book

3 brand-new titles to choose from each month

Available on the third Friday of every month
from WHSmith, ASDA, Tesco
and all good bookshops
www.millsandboon.co.uk

GEN/51/RTL11

Celebrate our centenary year with 24 special short stories!

ONLY £1.49! EACH

A special 100th Birthday Collection from your favourite authors including:

Penny Jordan • Diana Palmer • Lucy Gordon
Carole Mortimer • Betty Neels
Debbie Macomber • Sharon Kendrick
Alexandra Sellers • Nicola Cornick

Two stories published every month from January 2008 to January 2009

Collect all 24 stories to complete the set!

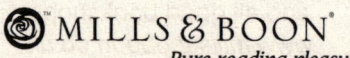

MILLS & BOON
Pure reading pleasure

www.millsandboon.co.uk